THE CORLEONE
FAMILY
COOKBOOK

THE CORLEONE
FAMILY
COOKBOOK

WRITTEN BY

Liliana Battle

PHOTOGRAPHS BY

Stacey Tyzzer

INSIGHT ◉ EDITIONS

San Rafael, California

CONTENTS

PARAMOUNT PICTURES PRESENTA

il Padrino

the Godfather®

Introduction

"Italians have a little joke, that the world is so hard a man must have two fathers to look after him, and that's why they have godfathers."

–Tom Hagen

Hailed as a masterpiece of cinema, the Godfather trilogy is an evocative and iconic exploration of Italian and Italian-American culture, especially the food. Directed by Francis Ford Coppola and based on the novel *The Godfather* by Italian-American author Mario Puzo, the first Godfather movie was released in 1972 and was an instant success, becoming one of the most critically acclaimed and highest-grossing movies of all time. Produced at a time when Italians were often depicted in film as lower-class, uneducated foreigners with heavy accents, *The Godfather* gave audiences a different perspective—a view from the inside of a mob family where the characters, even though involved with crime, were seen as immigrants in search of the American dream, with a fierce love for their families and a desire to give them the best life possible.

Some say the movies negatively present Italian-Americans as mobsters, but if you think the Godfather movies are just about a bunch of gangsters, you're missing the point. This is a story about a close-knit, loving family that just happens to be in the Mafia. The movies portray a deep sense of tradition and family where violence takes a secondary role to the pursuit of the American dream and taking care of the family, loving and protecting it at all costs. We sympathize and relate to the characters as we join them in good times and bad. We are drawn to the big family get-togethers where there is plenty of singing, dancing, laughter, and celebration, and, of course, food.

Food is central to the Godfather movies because it is at the table where families come together. Unlike most movies at the time, the films presented Italian food as more than the stereo-typical plump Italian housewife serving giant pots of tomato sauce. Whether it's the family sitting together eating bowls of pasta, lasagna, or chicken cacciatore, tables laden with a sumptuous array of food at a big celebration, or simple plates of cured meat, bread, cheese, and fruit to share (always with wine at the table to wash it down), the Godfather movies were instrumental in depicting Italian food as welcoming, abundant, and made to share. The family table is the center of everything; it's where people connect, and the criminal element in the movies somehow takes a back seat. "We don't discuss business at the table," says Sonny to Carlo when everyone sits down to eat. This is a time for family, a sacred place that can't be tainted.

Like many immigrants, the Corleone family kept their Sicilian roots alive by cooking the food from their homeland, passing on culinary traditions to future generations. That simple notion of breaking bread and sharing a meal together is the epitome of the Italian ethos. Italian food is generous and abundant and designed to be placed in the middle of the table for everyone to share. It breaks down barriers, encourages friendships, allows us to relax, sit down, and take time to listen to each other, and provides nourishment not only for the body, but also the soul. Food can transport us back to a time or a place. The aroma of a family meal ingrained in the senses reminds us of loved ones and special times together. Cooking is not just about filling empty stomachs; it's about coming together and creating memories. It's a bowl of "welcome to my family," a dish of "I care about you." It's love on a plate. Food is powerful, don't ever underestimate it.

There are many symbolic dishes throughout the Godfather movies. A box of cannoli that couldn't be left behind, a pot of pasta sauce made by a jolly Italian who just happens to be a hitman, a birthday cake that slices up an empire, veal Marsala followed by murder, and gnocchi that enflames a love affair. You will find all these recipes here. But you won't find any gimmicks, like a recipe for horse head (one of the first questions I was asked when people found out I was writing this book). Rest assured that the recipes in this book are delicious, authentic Italian and Italian-American recipes, inspired by the Corleone family and scenes from the movies, that you and your family will love to make and eat. The recipes encapsulate the Corleone family ethos as well as why I consider Italian food to be so good—it's made to share.

I hope you find many reasons to make these dishes and share them with your family as I have shared them with mine—and don't forget the wine. **Salute!**

The Italian Pantry

"Confidence is silent. Insecurities are loud."
–Vito Corleone

Being a confident cook takes more than following a good recipe. Just like it did for the Godfather, success comes from being prepared for whatever comes your way. Ever wondered how an Italian mamma can cook up a feast at a moment's notice without stressing out? The secret is a well-stocked pantry. Keep a stash of the following ingredients on hand at all times and you'll have everything you need to throw a delicious meal together with ease. Remember—Italian food is simple. A few staple ingredients cooked well. So, make sure your ingredients are top-notch.

OLIVE OIL

Of course, the most important ingredient in Italian cooking is olive oil. Vito Corleone knew that when he started his importing business, Genco Pura Olive Oil. Italian-made olive oil is hard to beat.

Regular olive oil: Use this for all cooking. It costs less than extra-virgin and won't impart a strong flavor to your food.

Extra-virgin olive oil: Use for salads, drizzle over food at the last minute, and serve with fresh bread for dunking. Flavor is everything here; buy the best you can afford.

Unless you use a lot of olive oil, don't be tempted to buy in bulk. Once opened, olive oil should be used within 6 to 8 weeks or it may turn rancid. Keep the oil stored in a dark place.

Many of the recipes in this book don't specify an exact amount of olive oil. The recipe may say "a splash," "a glug," or "a little." That's because no Italian would measure oil. The amount you need depends on the heat of the pan, how often you've tossed the vegetables, and all sorts of reasons why you need less or more. Italian cooking is as much about flavor as instinct. A glug or a splash means about 3 tablespoons or so, but don't measure it out. Just splash it in. If the pan looks dry, add a little more. Go with your gut.

FRYING OIL

Deep-frying requires oil to reach a high temperature. Use vegetable, sunflower, or rice-bran oil, all of which have a high smoking point, unlike olive oil.

VINEGAR

White wine vinegar is good for salads, but you can substitute red wine vinegar for a deeper flavor that is especially good with tomatoes. Balsamic vinegar, especially the good stuff from Modena, Italy, is delicious with a little olive oil and bread for simple antipasti.

GARLIC

If you don't have garlic, forget about cooking an Italian meal. There is no substitute for it. Buy bulbs with fat cloves and make sure they don't have any sprouts. The easiest way to peel a garlic clove is to lay a large knife sideways over the clove and whack down with the side of your fist. Good for letting out any frustrations and the skin will slide off easily.

ONIONS

Always keep onions in the pantry. They are the foundation of many Italian meals. Please, if a recipe asks for an onion and you don't have one, make something else. Please. It'll taste awful. Use simple, yellow onions for all cooking. Red onions are good for salads.

CANNED TOMATOES

Tomatoes are the backbone to any red Italian sauce. Why not fresh tomatoes? Because why bother? Buy the best canned tomatoes you can (of course the best ones use San Marzano tomatoes from Italy), and any Italian will tell you a can is as good as growing your own, with way less trouble. Save what's in your vegetable garden for salads or eating with bread and olive oil. You can buy canned tomatoes whole or already crushed. You get a little more flavor from the whole ones, but you will need to crush them yourself before adding to most recipes, so feel free to buy crushed tomatoes if that's easier for you.

PASSATA

Passata is pureed tomatoes, seeds and skin removed, available in jars at most supermarkets or gourmet stores. You can make your own by crushing cans of tomatoes and putting them through a food mill or sieve. Or replace with crushed tomatoes. It won't affect the flavor, but the texture won't be as smooth.

TOMATO PASTE

Adding tomato paste to a recipe gives a little oomph to the tomato flavor. It adds depth and strength. Recipes usually only need a small amount, so once you open a jar keep it in the fridge.

DRIED PASTA

If you have packets of pasta in your pantry, you can feed a family in next to no time.

Be careful with some cheaper varieties that can break up when they cook. Look for good-quality pasta made from durum wheat. If you can't eat wheat, don't worry, you don't have to miss out on a delicious bowl of pasta. Gluten-free varieties made with rice, corn, or quinoa flour are readily available at most supermarkets.

DRIED OREGANO

A visit to the supermarket spice aisle is overwhelming. There's so much to choose from. They all promise to release so many flavors—especially the so-called Italian herb mix. Forget about it! You only need one dried herb: oregano. That's it. If you can find the oregano that comes from Italy in branch form that you can crush yourself, please pay that little bit extra. It makes a phenomenal difference. But don't worry, any dried oregano is good. Throw out that Italian herb mix—trust me!

ANCHOVIES

If you're screwing up your nose, please, hear me out. Anchovies have got a bad rap. Oily, slimy, smelly little suckers (I can think of a few characters from the movies with similar characteristics)—most people don't like them. But, cooked down in a little olive oil with garlic, they bring incredibly salty (not fishy) flavor to a pasta dish. Pour over hot potatoes, brush over warm bread, or drizzle over a pizza. Add fresh herbs and you've got a great sauce to go with a piece of steak. Don't think of anchovies as fish, think of them as a punch of flavor.

DRIED CHILE FLAKES

If you like a little heat, it's as easy as shaking in some good-quality chile flakes. Remember, you can't take the heat out once it's in, so don't go crazy. Add in enough to get some heat, and put some in a bowl on the table for people who like things hot.

SALT AND PEPPER

Most of the recipes in this book don't specify amounts of pepper or salt. Pepper should be freshly ground—you can buy grinders with whole black peppercorns inside from most supermarkets. A good grinding means two to three turns of the grinder. Think of salt as the don, the backbone of the family. Salt is in almost every single recipe. Recipes will say "add salt to taste"—that's because I want you to taste everything. How do you know it's going be any good if you don't taste it first? Like chile flakes, salt can be added but not removed. So add a little at a time, taste, add more, and taste again. This is a lesson in Italian cooking—taste, taste, taste.

JARRED ANTIPASTI INGREDIENTS

Keep a variety of good-quality preserves in your pantry, and you can whip up a quick plate of antipasti or a simple pasta sauce in minutes. You can also add them to a pasta salad or use to top a pizza. Jars of olives, roasted bell peppers, sun-dried tomatoes, grilled eggplant, and marinated artichokes are all good choices.

CHICKEN STOCK

You can make your own Chicken Stock (page 41), and yes it does taste better if you do. But store-bought stock in the pantry can be a godsend on a cold winter's night when you want a big bowl of comfort. It is the foundation of many soup recipes and is essential in making risotto.

STRONG BREAD FLOUR

Of course, you need all the regular varieties of flour, but strong bread flour, often called bakers flour, is essential in making bread and pizza dough. It contains more protein and makes a big difference.

BREAD

Without bread on the table, is it really a meal? Most Italians would say no. Bread can be a meal in itself, made into sandwiches, or dipped into olive oil for a snack, but it is a must at the dinner table to *fare le scarpetta* (meaning "make a little shoe"), which is the Italian ritual of mopping up the sauce left in the bottom of the bowl. Bread is best eaten on the day it is made, so get friendly with your local baker if you don't want to make you own. An Italian would never throw away old bread—in fact some believe it is bad luck to do so. What do you do with stale bread? Slice it and toast it to make bruschetta, chop into cubes and bake to make croutons and add to salads, or tear it up and put it in the food processor to make bread crumbs. In Italian cooking, nothing is wasted.

OTHER ESSENTIAL INGREDIENTS

PARMESAN CHEESE

Whenever Parmesan cheese is mentioned in this book, I'm talking about the good stuff, Parmigiano Reggiano—the real deal—not that pregrated stuff you buy in a can or packet that has a distinct offensive aroma. Parmigiano Reggiano has a beautiful smell and flavor. Always buy Parmesan in a whole piece and grate fresh as needed. Serve in bowls for everyone to add as much or as little as they like. It's also delicious eaten on its own with fresh bread.

CURED MEAT

From prosciutto to pepperoni, there is a huge variety of Italian cold meat available, which, with a little bread, makes a quick meal for one or as many people as you need to feed. It is also great to add to pasta, salads, and sandwiches.

ITALIAN SAUSAGES

Fresh Italian sausages are the basis for many southern Italian meals. Full of spicy flavor, usually laced with fennel, bell pepper, oregano, and red wine, they are delicious cooked up and eaten with a little salad or a side of Pepperonata (page 149). They are essential in making Clemenza's Sauce (page 63), and who could say no to a serving of Sausages and Peppers (page 133) for a simple family meal.

You can buy Italian sausages from the supermarket, but an Italian butcher will give you the best money can buy.

EGGS

All eggs called for in this book are standard large size, about 2 ounces.

Antipasti

Antipasti is one of the most important Italian foods there is and is the most featured meal in all three Godfather movies. An assortment of cheese, bread, cured meats, fruits, and vegetables, it can be served in so many ways, for as few or as many people as you need. From a big spread for a large family celebration like Connie's wedding, to an impromptu casual lunch like the one Michael and Kate share in Sicily, to a small plate with a glass of wine over a business meeting, the tradition of antipasti ensures that a bite of something delicious is never too far away.

It's the easiest Italian meal to prepare. Just visit your local deli or supermarket, stock up on the best produce you can find, and lay it all out on a platter to share with friends or family. Along with a stash of Italian delicacies in your fridge and pantry, you can welcome anyone who drops by in the true Italian style.

Here's a guide to what to include—but you know what you like. Choose your favorites, buy what looks good, make sure you have variety, and you can't go wrong.

CURED MEAT

Cured meats such as prosciutto, mortadella, bresaola, coppa, lonza, sopressa, lardo, and capicola should be sliced as thin as possible (ask for it to be cut *fino fino*—very thin). Layer or drape onto the serving plate.

Other harder meats such as salami, pepperoni, cacciatore, and soppressata can be sliced into thin discs.

Try to include at least three varieties of meat, a mix of spicy and nonspicy. You will need at least three slices per person.

CHEESE

Either leave cheese in a wedge or cut into cubes, depending on how soft it is. A soft Gorgonzola dolce should be served in a wedge, whereas provolone can be cut into cubes. Pecorino could be left as a wedge or sliced—go with what makes sense for you.

Parmigiano Reggiano is the most traditional cheese to serve. Break into small chunks with a knife.

Fresh ricotta is delicious smeared onto bread with a little salt and a drizzle of olive oil.

One type of cheese works just as well as a variety. Just ensure there are roughly 2 to 3 ounces per person.

VEGETABLES

Sun-dried tomatoes, roasted bell peppers, grilled eggplant, olives, marinated mushrooms, and artichokes—all these can be bought from a store in jars.

Fresh tomatoes cut and drizzled with a little olive oil and sprinkled with salt are perfect with crusty bread. Homemade additions are worth the effort—try the Stuffed Mushrooms (page 157) or a bowl of Pepperonata (page 149). For a big celebration, you might want to add a bowl of Arancini (page 51).

FRESH FRUIT

Use grapes, pears, oranges, apricots, peaches, melon, berries, whatever is in season.

NUTS

Choose from almonds, walnuts, and Brazil nuts. Peanuts are perfect with a glass of ice-cold beer.

BREAD

Ciabatta is perfect, but any variety will be fine, as long as it's fresh. A small bowl with extra-virgin olive oil should always be on the table to dip your bread into. You could also add a little bowl of good balsamic vinegar.

GRISSINI

Grissini are thin, crispy breadsticks you can buy from the store. Or make your own (page 33).

Marinated Olives

You can pick up a container of marinated olives from a store, but they are quick and easy to make yourself. Any variety of olives will work in this recipe, and you can leave out the chile if you like.

One 10-ounce jar of olives in brine
1 teaspoon fresh rosemary
1 teaspoon dried oregano
1 sprig of fresh thyme
¼ teaspoon dried chile flakes
Peel of half a lemon, cut into strips
1 garlic clove, peeled and sliced
Olive oil

1. Drain the olives and then put them back into the jar. Add the rosemary, oregano, thyme, chile, lemon peel, and garlic. Pour enough olive oil into the jar to cover. Place the lid on the jar and shake well.

2. Set aside for at least 2 hours to marinate before serving. You can make this up to two weeks ahead. Keep covered in the refrigerator.

BREAD and PIZZA

"Give us this day our daily bread."
–Matthew 6:11

If you have bread on the table, you have a meal. Use it as Italians do—mop up the juices left on your plate, make a great sandwich, or simply serve with a bowl of olive oil for dipping, and a side of antipasti. Making bread is an art form; it takes time but is well worth it. There's nothing quite like the smell of fresh bread from the oven, but feel free to buy from your local baker if you don't have the time. No matter where you get your bread, don't ever throw away old bread. An Italian would regard that as a sin. Use leftover bread to make bruschetta or your own bread crumbs. Bread is life, don't waste it.

Pizza is one of the most beloved Italian meals. Whether you like your pizza thin and crispy or deep-dish, pizza symbolizes fast food—Italian style. Making your own pizza dough is easy, and homemade pizza is always better than what you buy from a chain store. Best of all, you can use the pizza dough to make calzone, pies, and even bread.

Ciabatta

Ciabatta is the most iconic Italian bread, and stars in almost every Godfather scene. Crispy on the outside, with a soft, airy crumb inside, and with a distinct chew, it is perfect with any meal. *Ciabatta* means "slipper" in Italian and is therefore the perfect bread to *fare le scarpetta* (meaning "make a little shoe"), which is the Italian custom of wiping up the dregs of sauce from the bottom of your plate. You can buy ciabatta from any bakery, but it is simple to make yourself. It takes a little time to rise, but there's something so satisfying in bringing something to the family table that you made by hand.

1¼ cups warm water

2 teaspoons dried yeast

1 teaspoon sugar

3¾ cups strong bread flour, plus extra flour for shaping

2 teaspoons salt

2 tablespoons olive oil

1. Pour the water into a small jug or bowl and add the yeast and sugar. Stir to combine and set aside for 5 to 10 minutes, or until foamy. This is a sign the yeast is activated. If the yeast doesn't foam it means it is dead and the bread won't rise.

2. Put the 3¾ cups of flour and salt into the bowl of a stand mixer fitted with a dough hook and mix until well incorporated. Pour in the water and yeast mixture and the olive oil and mix with a spatula to thoroughly combine. Use the dough hook attachment to knead the mixture for 5 to 8 minutes, or until smooth and shiny. You can do this by hand if you're up to it. Just mix with a spatula—but be warned, it's a bit of a work out! This is a wet dough, so don't be alarmed if it doesn't look like regular bread dough.

3. Transfer to a bowl that has been coated in a thin film of olive oil. Turn the dough over to coat. Cover with plastic wrap and leave to rise at room temperature for about 3 hours, or in the fridge for 10 to 12 hours, or until doubled in size. The longer prove will result in better flavor and texture, so if you have the time, let the dough do its thing in the fridge overnight.

4. Line a baking sheet with parchment paper and carefully tip the risen dough on top. Be gentle here, unlike normal bread dough that you punch down to eliminate air, this dough needs the air bubbles that have formed in order to produce the beautiful ciabatta texture once cooked. Use well-floured hands to gently coax the dough into a rough domed shape and leave a light film of flour all over the dough. Loosely cover and set aside for 30 minutes at room temperature.

5. Meanwhile, heat the oven to 400°F. Place a small baking dish on the bottom rack of the oven.

6. Place the rested dough on the baking sheet onto the oven rack directly above the baking dish you put in earlier. Tip a cup full of water into the empty baking dish and quickly shut the oven door. This creates steam, which helps the ciabatta obtain its distinct crust.

7. Cook for 35 minutes, or until dark golden, then remove the bread and allow it to cool as long as you can manage to keep yourself from ripping it apart and devouring it.

Salsiccia Sandwich

"You know the people like you, the press, the police, use words like Mafia, Cosa Nostra. This is a fantasy. The Italian-Americans are great people. We laid the bricks that built this city . . ."
–Joey Zasa, The Godfather Part III

Joey Zasa loved the fame that came with being a gangster and played up to the press at every opportunity, even making the front cover of *Time* magazine. As he walks with his entourage during the religious street festival in *The Godfather Part III* he stops and orders one of the most iconic Italian-American street foods there is, proudly telling the throng of press who surround him, "The salsiccia sandwiches are wonderful." This isn't any normal sandwich. We're talking Italian pork sausages, full of fennel, garlic, and herbs, stuffed into fresh bread with sautéed bell peppers. Salivating? You should be! Too bad for Joey, though. After he took a bite out of his sandwich he was chased down and shot dead by Vincent Mancini. Za za! At least he had a great last meal.

1. Cut bread in half, but not all the way through. Spoon in a generous serving of the warm sausage and pepper mixture.

SERVES 4 TO 6.

4 to 6 bread rolls
1 quantity Sausages and Peppers (page 133)

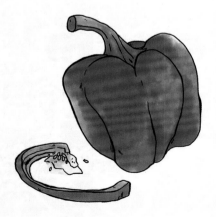

Bruschetta

You can use any variety of tomato here, but make sure they're juicy and ripe. Fresh homegrown tomatoes would be incredible—straight out of Vito Corleone's garden. One more thing, Italians pronounce it: *Brus-ketta*, not *Bru-shetta*.

1. Start by making the topping, ideally 30 minutes to 1 hour before serving, so the flavors have time to develop.

2. Chop the tomatoes into bite-size pieces and place into a large bowl. Add the onion, garlic, basil, olive oil, vinegar, and a good pinch of salt and toss to combine. Taste and add salt as needed.

3. Cook the slices of bread either on a grill plate, on a BBQ, or under a broiler until toasted and the edges are a little charred. Immediately rub one side with the peeled garlic clove. Drizzle with a little olive oil and either top generously with the tomato mixture or serve alongside for people to assemble their own.

SERVES 4 TO 8, DEPENDING ON SIZE OF BREAD USED.

TOPPING

16 ounces fresh ripe tomatoes (about 3 medium or 16 cherry tomatoes)

¼ red onion, finely chopped

1 large garlic clove, peeled and finely chopped

Small handful of fresh basil leaves, finely chopped

4 tablespoons extra-virgin olive oil

2 tablespoons red wine vinegar

Salt

BRUSCHETTE

4 to 8 slices homemade Ciabatta (page 23) or similar store bought (the amount you need depends on the size of the bread)

1 clove garlic, peeled

Olive oil

Pizza Dough

This is so much more than pizza dough. In true Italian style, Mamma would use one simple dough to make all kinds of different meals for her family. Once you learn this simple pizza dough recipe, you can use it to make everything from pizza to pies. If you have children who love to help in the kitchen, let them help knead the dough and then punch it down after it rises. Cooking with children is a perfect way to create family memories.

1. Pour the water into a bowl and add the sugar and yeast. Stir. Set aside for 5 to 10 minutes, or until foamy. This is a sign the yeast has activated. If the mixture doesn't look foamy on the surface, it means the yeast is dead, and the dough won't work.

2. Mix the flour and salt in a large bowl. Make a well in the center and add the yeast mixture and the olive oil. Mix together, then knead, either with an electric mixer using the dough hook or on a floured surface with your hands, until you have a smooth ball of dough that springs back when you touch it.

3. Drizzle a little olive oil into a large bowl and place the ball of dough inside. Turn to slick a little olive oil all over, then cover and allow to sit in a warm place for 1 hour, or until the dough has doubled in size. The time this takes will vary depending on the temperature in the room. You can even put it in the fridge and let it rise slowly overnight if you like (a slow rise actually improves the flavor).

4. Once the dough has doubled in size, punch it down with your fist to deflate the air, and knead for a couple of minutes on a lightly floured surface. The dough is now ready to be used. This recipe makes enough for two large pizzas. If you have any dough left over, wrap it in plastic wrap and freeze for up to 3 months. Defrost prior to using.

1½ cups warm water
1 teaspoon sugar
2 teaspoons dried yeast
5 cups strong bread flour
1 teaspoon salt
2 tablespoons olive oil

Thin and Crispy Pizza

No matter how much you love cooking, there's always time for takeout. In the first movie, the Corleone family lived near Chinatown, and in the scene where the guys are waiting for the phone call to find out where Michael is going to meet with Sollozzo and McCluskey, they are sitting around the table eating Chinese takeout. Even Italians order takeout. One of the most common Italian takeout meals is pizza, and there's nothing wrong with ordering up a pizza or two when there are other things on your mind besides cooking. But homemade pizzas are simple to make yourself and a great way to get the family together. Have a pizza night and get everyone to add his or her favorite toppings. A few beers or a glass of wine, and it's a great night in.

1. Place a pizza stone or large baking sheet on the middle rack in the oven and preheat to its hottest setting at least 30 minutes before you need to cook the pizzas. Pizzas cook best at high temperature; putting the dough directly onto a hot surface encourages a crispy crust. If you have apizza oven, heat to manufacturer's instructions. If you are lucky enough to own an outdoor wood-fired oven, stoke it up. (If you own one of these you'll know what to do.)

2. Split the dough into two pieces. Tear a piece of parchment, roughly the size of your baking sheet or pizza stone, and lay on a flat surface. Place one piece of dough onto the parchment and roll the dough to a rough round shape as thin as you can get it, leaving parchment overhanging on the edges.

3. Spread sauce evenly on the dough, leaving a ¾-inch edge, and then top with the other ingredients. Carefully lift the pizza using the overhanging parchment paper straight into the oven onto the heated pizza stone or baking sheet. If the oven is hot enough, the pizza will only take 5 to 10 minutes to cook. However, because all ovens are different, go by eye. The dough should be crisp, golden, and puffy, and the cheese should be bubbling.

4. Carefully remove the pizza from the oven, slice, and serve.

5. Repeat with the remaining dough.

HERE ARE TWO CLASSIC VARIETIES:

1 quantity Pizza Dough (page 28)

MARGHERITA
½ cup Tomato Sauce (page 59 or store bought)
4 ounces (1 cup) mozzarella cheese, grated, or 1 large ball of fresh mozzarella
8 fresh basil leaves

PEPPERONI
½ cup Tomato Sauce (page 59 or store bought)
1 teaspoon dried oregano
¼ cup pepperoni, thinly sliced
4 ounces (1 cup) mozzarella cheese, grated

Sicilian Pizza

Comparing a Sicilian pizza to a regular pizza is like comparing Mamma Corleone to Hyman Roth's wife, Marcia. One is going to give you a big bowl of spaghetti; the other is going to give you a tuna sandwich. Now, I'm not saying there's anything wrong with a good tuna sandwich, just like there's nothing wrong with a thin and crispy pizza. But this home-style pizza is thicker and heartier than regular pizza, almost breadlike, oozing with cheese, and it gives you that warm and satisfying feeling just like Mamma's food should.

1. Roll the pizza dough on a lightly floured surface into a large rectangle, about 13 by 18 inches (don't be too precise here, this is a rustic style pizza). Coat the base of a baking sheet of about the same size with olive oil and place the dough on top, stretching it as best you can to cover the base of the baking sheet. Brush or spray the top with olive oil, cover, and set aside for 1 hour, or until risen and puffy.

2. Thirty minutes before cooking, preheat the oven to very hot, 500°F.

3. Cover the pizza dough with the sliced mozzarella, then sprinkle Parmesan cheese over evenly. Spoon the sauce evenly over the top, then add the grated mozzarella and oregano.

4. Bake for 15 minutes or until the dough is golden underneath. Check by using a spatula to look underneath.

5. Cut into slices and serve.

SERVES 6.

1 quantity Pizza Dough (page 28)
Olive oil
1 pound mozzarella cheese, thinly sliced
3 ounces (1 cup) Parmesan cheese, grated
1 cup Tomato Sauce (page 59 or store bought)
4 ounces (1 cup) mozzarella, extra, grated
1 tablespoon dried oregano

Grissini

Family traditions and a connection to their Sicilian roots are important in the Corleone family. In all Italian families, children are welcomed into the kitchen from a young age. They become a part of the conversations and relationships that generate while cooking together, instilling in them the importance of making a meal for the family. The kitchen is where everyone comes together. Rolling out the grissini is just like rolling play-dough and is perfect to get the kids involved in the kitchen. grissini are delicious wrapped in paper-thin prosciutto or served alongside a selection of antipasti.

Note: You only need a half quantity of Pizza Dough (page 28) here; simply freeze the other half to use for another day.

MAKES ABOUT 20.

½ quantity Pizza Dough (page 28)
2 tablespoons fennel seeds
2 tablespoons sea salt flakes
Olive oil

1. Preheat oven to 400°F. Line a large baking sheet with parchment.

2. Roll the dough out onto a lightly floured surface into a rectangle about ¼ inch thick. Cut into strips, about ½ inch wide. Sprinkle with the fennel seeds and salt, then use your hand to roll each strip into a thin log shape.

3. Place the grissini onto your prepared baking sheets and brush the tops with olive oil. Cover and allow to rise slightly—for 15 minutes.

4. Bake for 30 minutes, or until golden and crisp.

5. Cool and either serve or store in an airtight container for up to 1 week.

Calzone

A calzone is basically a folded pizza, designed to eat on the go, and most commonly bought from street stalls, like in the street festival in *The Godfather Part III.* Calzone literally means "trouser leg" and may have gotten its name because calzones are the perfect snack to eat while walking around, perfect for the boys walking the streets keeping an eye on the neighborhood.

MAKES 6.

1 quantity Pizza Dough (page 28)

½ cup Tomato Sauce (page 59 or store bought)

8 ounces sliced pepperoni or other salami

1 tablespoon dried oregano

1 ounce (⅓ cup) Parmesan cheese, grated

4 ounces (1 cup) mozzarella cheese, grated

Small handful of fresh basil leaves, roughly chopped

1 egg

1. Preheat the oven to very hot, 500°F. Line a large baking sheet with parchment.

2. Divide the dough into 6 pieces. Roll each piece into a thin circle. Spoon some sauce onto one half of each round, leaving a ½-inch border. Evenly distribute the salami or pepperoni over the sauce. Sprinkle with oregano, then the Parmesan and mozzarella cheese. Scatter over the fresh basil.

3. Whisk the egg with 1 tablespoon of water and brush onto the border. Fold the dough over and press the edges to seal. Cut a small slash with a knife on the tops to allow the steam to escape as they cook, and brush all over with remaining egg wash.

4. Place onto the prepared baking sheet and cook for 15 minutes, or until golden and crisp.

5. Eat while hot.

Pizza Pie

Dean Martin, one of the most beloved Italian-American singers of all time, sang about the moon and love and a big pizza pie. No question he would have performed at one of the Corleone family casinos in the 1970s; his name even appears on a billboard in Vegas in *The Godfather Part II*. I'm sure they made him an offer he couldn't refuse.

This pizza pie, or *pizza rustica* as it's known in Italy, is exactly what its name suggests—a pizza turned into a pie. It's got everything in it—cheese, plenty of salty salami, bacon, Italian sausage, herbs, and garlic—all wrapped up in pizza dough. I have to agree with Dean Martin, there's plenty to love about a pizza pie. That's amore! This pie is perfect family food, and leftovers make a great lunch the next day.

1. Put the sausage meat, bacon, and onion into a frying pan with a little olive oil and cook over medium-high heat, stirring often until meat is cooked, bacon is crisp, and onions are translucent. Add the garlic and cook for another minute, stirring. Set aside to cool completely.

2. Preheat the oven to 400°F.

3. In a large bowl, combine the ricotta, mozzarella, provolone, Parmesan, pepperoni or salami, parsley, basil, oregano, a good pinch of salt, a grinding of black pepper, and the cooled meat mixture. Lightly beat 3 of the eggs and add them to the mixture. Stir to thoroughly combine.

4. Cut the pizza dough into two pieces, one slightly larger than the other. Roll out the larger piece onto a lightly floured surface to fit a round 10-inch pie dish with a 1-inch overhang. Transfer into your pie dish. Add the filling and smooth the top so that it is even.

5. Now roll out the second piece of dough, large enough to cover the top. Transfer to the top of the pie and use your fingers to pinch the overhanging pastry inward to seal. Make a couple of slashes in the top with a sharp knife to allow steam to escape.

6. Whisk the last egg with 1 tablespoon of water and brush all over the top of the pie.

7. Bake for 15 minutes, then lower the temperature to 300°F, and cook for another 40 minutes, or until the crust is golden and crisp.

8. Allow to cool for 30 minutes before slicing and serving. This pie is best served warm or at room temperature.

SERVES 6 TO 8.

17 ounces fresh Italian sausage, casings removed

8 ounces rindless bacon, chopped

½ onion, peeled and diced

Olive oil

2 cloves garlic, peeled and finely chopped

15 ounces ricotta, drained

1 cup mozzarella cheese, grated

1 cup provolone cheese, grated

1 ounce (⅓ cup) Parmesan cheese, grated

8 ounces pepperoni or other salami, diced

Small handful of fresh parsley leaves, chopped

Small handful of fresh basil leaves, chopped

1 tablespoon dried oregano

Salt

Freshly ground black pepper

4 eggs

1 quantity Pizza Dough (page 28)

SOUP and RISOTTO

"A man who doesn't spend time with his family can never be a real man."
–Vito Corleone

A bowl of warm soup or risotto is perfect comfort food. It is worth making your own stock for the best flavor, but you can buy excellent stock from supermarkets these days, so it is a good idea to always keep some on hand for a last-minute meal. Soups and risotto are very versatile, and you can add anything you've got lurking around your kitchen to boost the flavor. A little leftover chicken can be added to risotto, or any tired-looking vegetables can be transformed into a killer minestrone.

There is only one risotto recipe here, simply because it is open to your own interpretation. Add a little leftover cooked chicken or extra vegetables as you please. The method is the same. Don't be put off by making your own risotto the proper way—adding stock gradually and stirring as you go. It takes a little extra effort than other methods, but the result is a creamy bowl of goodness, still with a little bite, that you will love. Perfect it and you will be the envy of other home cooks, especially when you turn leftovers into mouthwatering Arancini (page 51)!

Chicken Stock

Relax, you don't have to make your own stock. You can buy perfectly good stock from the store. But if you have a little time, homemade stock is just that little bit tastier, and it's really simple to make. Plus, it's healthier because store-bought stocks often contain a lot of salt.

1. Put all the ingredients into a large pot. Cover with water, about 6½ quarts, and cook over high heat until the water comes to a boil. Reduce heat to low, cover, and simmer for 2 hours, stirring every now and then. A grayish foam will float to the top as the stock cooks; skim this off as it cooks.

2. Strain through a fine sieve and discard the solids. Pour into an airtight container and refrigerate overnight.

3. The next day, remove the top layer of fat that has solidified. Discard.

4. Store the chicken stock in an airtight container in the refrigerator for 5 days or freeze for up to 6 months. If freezing, you may want to separate into smaller containers.

MAKES ABOUT 4 QUARTS.

4½ pounds chicken carcasses, or leg and wing pieces

2 onions, peeled and chopped

3 carrots, peeled and chopped

3 celery sticks, peeled and chopped

2 garlic cloves, peeled and bruised (squashed)

2 bay leaves

1 tablespoon salt

Mamma's Chicken Soup

Italian mammas serve this simple, yet comforting soup as medicine. When you're not feeling well, when you're upset, or any time you need that extra bit of love, whip some up. Every Italian child grows up calling it "pastina," which is actually the name of the little star-shaped pasta most often used (also called "stelline").

1. Heat a saucepan over low-medium heat and add the onion, carrot, and celery, with a splash of olive oil. Cook, stirring frequently, for 5 minutes or until the vegetables have softened. Add the chicken wings and cook for another minute, turning the chicken over to brown on both sides. Pour in the chicken stock, increase the heat, and bring to a boil. Cover, reduce the heat to low, and simmer for 30 minutes. Skim any fat or foam that rises to the surface and discard.

2. Take the chicken out of the pot and remove the meat from the bones. Discard the chicken skin and bones, shred the meat, and return to the pot. Increase the heat and bring back to a boil. Add the pasta and cook until the pasta is soft, about 5 minutes, depending on the type of pasta.

3. Taste and add salt as necessary.

4. Serve hot with crusty bread and a grating of Parmesan if desired.

SERVES 6.

1 onion, peeled and finely chopped

2 carrots, peeled and finely chopped

2 sticks of celery, peeled and finely sliced

Olive oil

12 chicken wings

2 quarts (8 cups) Chicken Stock (above or store bought)

1 cup small pasta (such as orzo, pastina, or ditalini)

Salt

Minestrone

The best way to describe minestrone is family. It's warm, comforting, packed with everything and anything, a big mixture of personalities and flavors somehow fused together into something beautiful, made to share. The acidic flavors counteract the bland, and lighter, fresh flavors balance the stronger aromas. This soup has texture, guts, and substance. Some ingredients seem to dominate the others, but it is the less powerful ingredients that really make all the difference. This soup is full of goodness. It is never the same, yet it is always cohesive—and it always works, even if you need to taste and adjust, tweak, and allow the flavors time to meld and support each other, making the whole better than any one of the ingredients on its own, with the strength of the tomato broth holding it all together. Just like the Corleone family.

This recipe is a starting point for you to add in whatever you have. The zucchini can be replaced with green beans, cauliflower, broccoli, more carrot and celery, or similarly textured vegetables. You can even add small diced potatoes if you like, and any type of canned beans will do.

1. Put the carrots, celery, onion, and a good splash of olive oil into a large pot. Cook over medium heat for 5 minutes, or until vegetables are tender. Add the garlic and cook, stirring for another minute.

2. Add the chicken stock, zucchini, canned tomatoes, cabbage, oregano, a good pinch of salt, and a grinding of black pepper, and stir to combine. Increase the heat and bring to a boil, then cover with a lid, reduce heat, and simmer for 30 minutes.

3. Taste and add seasoning if necessary. If too thick, add a little water. Increase the heat and bring back to a boil, tip in the pasta, and cook until pasta is almost cooked, around 5 minutes (depending on which kind of pasta is used). Add the fresh herbs, greens, and cannellini beans, stir through, and cook for another minute or until greens have wilted and pasta is soft.

4. Serve with crusty bread.

SERVES 6 TO 8.

2 carrots, peeled and chopped into large chunks

3 sticks of celery, peeled and chopped

1 onion, peeled and finely chopped

Olive oil

2 garlic cloves, peeled and finely sliced

6 cups Chicken Stock (page 41 or store bought)

1 zucchini, chopped

Three 14½-ounce cans of diced tomatoes

1 cup shredded cabbage

1 teaspoon dried oregano

Salt

Freshly ground black pepper

2 cups medium-sized pasta (such as shells, elbows, or macaroni)

Small handful of fresh parsley, chopped

Small handful of fresh basil leaves, chopped

1 cup greens, chopped (such as spinach, cavolo nero, or kale)

One 14½-ounce can of cannellini beans, drained and rinsed

Pasta e Fagioli

In *The Godfather Part II* we see Vito and his wife Carmela starting their lives together in a humble apartment on Tenth Avenue, in New York City. Vito earned a meager living working for Genco Abbandando at his grocery store. (Genco and Vito later partner in the olive oil business: Genco Pura Olive Oil Importing.) With a young family and not much money, Vito was lucky his young wife was a skilled cook and always found a way to feed her family from very little.

Pasta e fagioli is a typical peasant dish that is economical to make but hearty enough to feed a family. I doubt Carmela would have had the money to add the pancetta back then, and it can be made successfully without it. But it adds a salty depth of flavor that brings this humble soup to another level.

1. Put the pancetta or bacon, onion, and a splash of olive oil into a pot and cook over medium-high heat, stirring often, until the onions are tender. Add the garlic and cook, stirring, for another minute.

2. Increase the heat and add the passata, water, a good pinch of salt, grinding of black pepper, and the chile flakes. Stir to combine and bring to a boil.

3. Reduce the heat, add the cannellini beans, and stir to combine. Cover and simmer for 30 minutes. Add the fresh basil leaves, stir through, and cook for another 5 minutes. Taste and season as needed.

4. Meanwhile, bring a large pot of salted water to a boil, tip in the pasta, and stir with a wooden spoon. Cook until the pasta is al dente, then drain and immediately add to the fagioli sauce in the pot. Stir to combine.

5. Ladle into bowls, drizzle with a little olive oil, and serve with grated Parmesan if desired.

SERVES 4 TO 6.

7 ounces pancetta or streaky bacon, finely chopped

½ onion, peeled and finely diced

Olive oil

2 garlic cloves, peeled and finely sliced

24 ounces passata (pureed tomatoes, page 14)

1 cup water

Salt

Freshly ground black pepper

½ teaspoon dried chile flakes

Two 14½-ounce cans of cannellini beans, drained and rinsed

Small handful of fresh basil leaves

3 cups (10½ ounces) short pasta (such as shells, macaroni, or penne)

Wedding Soup

The name of this soup may suggest it is most often served at weddings, and indeed it would make a beautiful starter to celebrate the first meal as husband and wife. But the name actually comes from its Italian name: *minestra maritata*, which means "married soup" referring to the marriage of contrasting ingredients—the fresh green leafy vegetables and the hearty meat flavor from the meatballs. In that case it would have made a perfect dish for Connie and Carlo's wedding, which saw the marriage of Connie, young, fresh, fragile, and weak, to Carlo who uses his masculine force and power to control her. But unlike their marriage destined for failure, this soup is a triumph and perfect for any occasion.

1. Form the raw meatball mixture into small balls, about 1 inch in diameter. You can make them any size you like really, but they are nicer served a bit smaller than normal in this soup.

2. Brown the meatballs briefly in olive oil in a skillet. They don't need to cook all the way through at this stage, just nice and golden on the outside. Drain on paper towels.

3. Splash some olive oil into a large pot and add the onion, carrots and celery. Cook over medium-high heat, stirring often, until vegetables are tender. Add the garlic and cook for another minute. Add the wine and allow to boil for a minute, then add the chicken stock, increase the heat, and bring to a boil.

4. Carefully add the meatballs and the pasta and cook for 10 minutes, or until the pasta is almost done and the meatballs are cooked through. Taste and add salt as needed.

5. Finally, add the oregano and leafy greens, stir gently, and cook for another 2 minutes or until greens have wilted.

6. Ladle the soup into bowls, and sprinkle grated Parmesan on top.

SERVES 6.

1 quantity Meatball mixture (page 63)

Olive oil

1 onion, peeled and diced

2 carrots, peeled and diced

2 celery sticks, peeled and diced

1 garlic clove, peeled and finely diced

½ cup white wine

8 cups Chicken Stock (page 41 or store bought)

¾ cup (2¾ ounces) small pasta (such as ditalini, orzo, or acini di pepe)

1 tablespoon dried oregano

8 ounces leafy green vegetables, trimmed and chopped (such as spinach or escarole)

Salt

Parmesan cheese, grated

Risotto Milanese

"I respect those that tell me the truth, no matter how hard it is."
–Michael Corleone

I'm not going to lie to you, making a pot of risotto to feed a family is much trickier than making a bowl of pasta. It requires your full attention as you stand at the pot and add the stock gradually while you stir continuously for 20 minutes. But, please, don't let that put you off. This simple, creamy risotto is the perfect side dish, especially with Osso Buco (page 131), and any leftovers can be made into Arancini (page 51), which is reason enough to make it in the first place.

1. Pour the chicken stock into a medium saucepan with the saffron threads and place over high heat. Bring to a boil, then reduce to a low simmer and keep warm.

2. Splash a little olive oil and 2 tablespoons of the butter into a heavy pan and cook the onion over medium heat until translucent. Add the garlic and cook for another minute, stirring to ensure the garlic doesn't burn.

3. Add the rice and stir for 30 seconds to gently toast the rice and coat in the oil. Add the wine and cook, stirring, until the wine has evaporated.

4. Reduce the heat to medium-low and add a ladleful of the warm stock. Stir and allow the stock to almost completely absorb into the rice before adding another ladleful of warm stock. Keep doing this, adding stock, stirring until it's absorbed, adding another ladleful, etc., until almost all the liquid has been absorbed and the rice is just tender (about 20 minutes).

5. Remove from the heat and toss in the Parmesan and remaining butter. Stir vigorously to incorporate. Season with salt to taste.

SERVES 4 TO 6.

4½ cups Chicken Stock (page 41 or store bought)
½ teaspoon saffron threads
Olive oil
5 tablespoons butter
1 onion, peeled and finely diced
2 garlic cloves, peeled and finely chopped
2 cups arborio rice
½ cup white wine
½ cup Parmesan cheese, grated
Salt

Arancini

Arancini means "little oranges" in Italian, and they are a popular street food in Sicily. Contrary to their name, they don't contain oranges at all, but are so named because of their appearance. Golden and round, just like a small orange.

Oranges are very significant in the Godfather movies. Almost every time tragedy is about to strike you will see an orange somewhere in the scene. From Vito Corleone getting shot and oranges spilling onto the street, to the pile of oranges at the dinner table when Tom Hagen meets with Jack Woltz (we all know what happens to his horse after that meeting), to Don Fanucci picking up an orange from a street stall as he walks to his apartment where Vito shoots him, to the oranges that roll off the table when the helicopter comes in to assassinate the leaders of the families in *The Godfather Part III*, and of course, the segments of orange the Don places in his mouth to play with his grandson before he dies in his tomato patch. There are so many instances; watch the movies again and you will find many more.

MAKES ABOUT 30.

4 cups Risotto Milanese (page 49), cooled

6 eggs

1½ cups Parmesan cheese, grated

Salt

2 cups all-purpose flour

3 cups dried breadcrumbs

7 ounces mozzarella cheese, cut into ⅓-inch cubes

Oil, for frying

1. Put the risotto into a large bowl. Whisk 2 of the eggs briefly and add them to the risotto with 1 cup of the Parmesan cheese and a good pinch of salt. Mix to combine thoroughly. The rice should stick together when squished with your hands. This depends on how sticky your risotto was to begin with, so if you find it a little dry just add one more egg and mix again.

2. Set up your crumbing station. Crack the remaining 4 eggs into a bowl and add ⅓ cup water. Whisk to combine. Place the flour into a separate bowl and the bread crumbs mixed with the remaining Parmesan into a third.

3. Take a small handful of the risotto mixture (about ⅓ cup) and flatten it slightly in the palm of your hand. Place a cube of mozzarella in the center and then cup your hand to mold the risotto around the cube of cheese to form a ball shape. This is messy work, and your hands are the best utensils here. Wetting your hands every now and then as you go prevents your hands from becoming too gluggy and encourages the rice to mold in place. The balls should be roughly the size of golf balls.

4. Once all the balls are formed, roll each one into the flour, then dip into the egg mixture, then finally into the bread crumbs, rolling to coat.

5. At this stage the arancini can be refrigerated for one day, or placed into an airtight container, in single layers separated by greaseproof paper, and frozen for up to three months. Defrost prior to frying.

6. Fill a deep fryer or large pot halfway with oil. Heat to 360°F. Drop the arancini into the oil in batches, about 8 at a time. Fry for 4 minutes, or until golden and crisp. Serve hot for the full molten cheesy center effect.

PASTA

**"A friend should always underestimate your virtues
and an enemy overestimate your faults."**
–Vito Corleone

Pasta is the backbone to Italian cooking. In almost every scene in the Godfather movies when the Corleone family sits at the table, they are eating pasta. This is not simply a stereotype, this is how Italians eat. My own father ate pasta every night of his life. Pasta is the basis of so many meals; it adds substance to a soup and can be accompanied by hearty meat sauces or light fresh ingredients. The perfect blank canvas, pasta can be whatever you want it to be.

Pasta Basics

FRESH OR DRIED? If you think a true Italian always makes homemade pasta you're wrong. Sure, fresh is beautiful, especially for special occasions, but most of time they use good-quality dried pasta and always have at least a few varieties in the pantry, ready to turn into a family meal.

Most recipes can use any kind of pasta you have on hand, but generally the long, thin noodles, such as linguine, pair well with light herb- and oil-based sauces; thicker noodles like spaghetti are good all-arounders, great with tomato-based or creamy sauces; wider noodles, such as pappardelle, are good for meatier sauces that need more pasta per bite. The shorter shapes, such as rigatoni and fusilli, have ridges and twists designed to encourage the sauce to cling, and tubes like ziti and penne are designed to trap the sauce. When choosing what kind of pasta to use, think about how heavy the sauce is and pair with a shape that has a thickness that will give the best balance of pasta to sauce.

GOLDEN RULES FOR COOKING PASTA:

- Pasta needs room to cook. Don't crowd it in a small pot of water; it will clump together, and you'll end up with a mess. A big pot, like a stockpot, is the best equipment. You will need 5 to 6 quarts of water for 14 ounces of pasta.

- Once the water is boiling, add a generous pinch of salt, don't be shy. Most of the salt is left in the water after the pasta has drained, but without salt, the pasta has no taste.

- Add the pasta and immediately give it a good stir. This ensures it won't stick together—do not add olive oil to the water!

- Cook, stirring every now and then, until al dente (literally meaning "to the tooth"—still with a little bite). Cooking time depends on the type of pasta used, so you can read the manufacturer's instructions on the back of the packet, but really the best way to tell if pasta is done is to keep an eye on it, stir every now and then, and take some out and taste it yourself. Fresh pasta cooks more quickly than dried and tends to be softer in texture.

- Always reserve a little of the cooking water—it contains starch that is sometimes needed to add moisture and body to a sauce. Just scoop some out with a cup before you drain the pasta.

- Always dress cooked pasta with sauce straight away. If left to sit, it will cling together like glue.

- Pasta (unless it's a baked pasta like lasagna) waits for no one. So, make sure everyone is sitting at the table ready to eat when the pasta is almost ready. There's nothing more disappointing than a cold bowl of pasta.

Fresh Pasta Dough

Fresh pasta is worth the time and effort. It somehow seems more luxurious than dried pasta. It may seem daunting, but actually it's simple to make, and you may find the process of kneading, rolling, and shaping the dough quite therapeutic. Best of all, if you're in the mood you can make more than you need and stash it in the freezer for many delicious meals to come. This is the easiest recipe to remember (and easier to make than you think): 1 egg per person and 3½ ounces of flour for every egg. Simple.

TO MAKE ENOUGH FOR 4 SERVINGS:

14 ounces flour
4 eggs

1. You can tip the flour straight onto your kitchen counter if you like, or into a mixing bowl. Make a well in the center and crack the eggs in. Using either your fingers or a fork, whisk the eggs gently, slowly incorporating a little flour into the center as you go. Once you have what looks like a shaggy mess, squish it together and knead on a lightly floured surface until the dough feels soft and smooth (about 10 minutes). If you are finding the dough a bit sticky, dust with a little more flour. If the dough feels too tough, drizzle with a little olive oil. Rely on your instincts here—sometimes the temperature of the room can affect how the dough comes together, so go with your senses.

2. Wrap in plastic wrap and allow to rest for 30 minutes.

3. You will need a pasta machine to roll out the dough. Of course, you can use a rolling pin, but it is very hard work (respect to all the nonni out there who have always rolled by hand), and pasta machines are not expensive so it's well worth the small investment.

4. Cut the dough into 6 portions. Work with one portion at a time, leaving the rest covered so it doesn't dry out.

5. Take one portion of dough and flatten slightly with your hands. Dust lightly in flour. Set the rollers on your pasta machine to the first (largest) setting. Feed the dough through the pasta machine, then fold in half and feed through again. Do this eight times on the first setting, dusting with more flour if the dough seems sticky. This step is called "laminating" and ensures the pasta becomes velvety and smooth.

6. Turn the knob on the pasta machine to the next setting and feed the dough through once. Now set the machine to the next setting and repeat. As you keep turning the knob, the roller becomes thinner, and the dough becomes thinner and longer. The higher the number, the thinner and

more fragile the pasta sheet will become. Depending on what you are making, you can make your pasta sheet as thick or thin as you like. Generally, you will want very thin sheets for making filled pasta, such as ravioli, because you will be sticking two sheets together, and you'll want about the third- or fourth-to-last settings for most other pasta shapes. This is personal taste, so experiment and go with what you like.

7. You can now cut the sheets into whatever shape you like. A knife is as good a tool as any, but you can also use a pastry wheel, or feed through the pasta machine with a cutting attachment—most have one that cuts the sheets into long strands of spaghetti or fettuccine. Make sure you dust the sheet with flour before doing this, so the strands don't stick together.

8. Once cut, toss your pasta generously with flour and let dry at room temperature on trays or on a clean surface. Long strands should be formed into little mounds, or nests, to make them easier to pick up later.

9. You can cook the pasta straight away, but it's easiest to make in advance, so once it's dry, place in the freezer on trays. After the pasta is frozen, transfer to airtight containers or snap lock bags. When ready to cook, just add the frozen pasta straight to boiling salted water.

10. Fresh pasta is more delicate to cook than dried. Sometimes it is best to scoop it out of the water with a slotted spoon, rather than dump it into a colander—especially filled pasta which may break.

Tomato Sauce

Every Italian knows how to make their own tomato sauce. It is the foundation of many meals and worth making extra so you're always prepared.

1. Splash the olive oil into a saucepan and add the onion, celery, and carrot. Cook over medium heat, stirring often, until vegetables are tender. Add a little extra olive oil if the mixture seems dry. Add the garlic and cook another minute.

2. Pour in the tomatoes. There is always a residue left in the bottom of the can, so add a little water to loosen, swirl it around, and add that to the pot too (about ½ cup of water total). Add the oregano, sugar, and a good pinch of salt, and stir to combine. Increase the heat and bring to a boil. Cover, reduce the heat to low, and simmer for 30 minutes.

3. Add the basil leaves, taste, and add more salt if needed. Cook, uncovered, for another 15 minutes.

4. Either use a stick blender or transfer the sauce to a food processor and blend to a smooth consistency. This sauce can be refrigerated in an airtight container for a week, or frozen for up to 6 months.

MAKES ABOUT 2½ QUARTS.

3 tablespoons olive oil

1 onion, peeled and finely chopped

1 celery stick, finely chopped

½ carrot, peeled and finely chopped

3 garlic cloves, peeled and finely chopped

Six 14½-ounce cans crushed tomatoes

½ cup water

¾ tablespoon dried oregano

1 teaspoon sugar

Salt

5 fresh basil leaves

Bolognese Sauce

Bolognese sauce is the base of great lasagna but can also be served with any pasta for a meaty, hearty dish the whole family will love. Make sure you don't use extra-lean meat as the fat adds flavor.

1. Heat the olive oil in a large pot and add the onion, celery, and carrot. Cook over medium heat, stirring often, until vegetables are tender. Add the garlic and stir for another minute, then add the tomato paste and cook for one more minute.

2. Increase heat to high and add the ground beef. Cook, stirring, to brown the beef all over. Add the oregano, a good pinch of salt, and a grinding of black pepper, and stir to combine.

3. Add tomatoes, passata, and the water—tip the water into the empty cans and slosh around to remove any tomato residue and pour in. Stir, and bring to a boil. Add the bay leaves and sugar, cover, and reduce heat. Simmer for 1 hour. Uncover, increase heat to low-medium and cook for 30 minutes.

4. Taste and add salt as necessary. Throw in the basil leaves and cook for another 15 minutes, or until sauce has thickened. If you are using the sauce to make lasagna, it doesn't need to be too thick. If you are serving over pasta, let it cook a little longer to reduce a little more; the longer it cooks the better it tastes (but use common sense here and don't let it burn). Once cooked, remove the bay leaves and discard.

5. Sauce can be refrigerated for up to 3 days, or frozen for up to 6 months.

MAKES ABOUT 2½ QUARTS.

¼ cup olive oil

1 onion, peeled and finely diced

1 celery stick, peeled and finely sliced

1 carrot, peeled and finely diced

3 garlic cloves, peeled and finely sliced

3 tablespoons tomato paste

2½ pounds ground beef

1 tablespoon dried oregano

Salt

Freshly ground black pepper

Four 14½-ounce cans crushed tomatoes

1 cup water

24 ounces passata (pureed tomatoes, page 14)

2 bay leaves

1 teaspoon sugar

4 basil leaves

Clemenza's Sauce

"Hey, come over here kid, learn something. You never know, you might have to cook for twenty guys someday. You see, you start out with a little bit of oil. Then you fry some garlic. Then you throw in some tomatoes, tomato paste, you fry it, ya make sure it doesn't stick. You get it to a boil, you shove in all your sausage and meatballs, hey? And a little bit o' wine. An' a little bit o' sugar, and that's my trick."

—Clemenza

Even in times of crisis, people need to eat. This recipe is adapted from the scene in *The Godfather* when Clemenza teaches Michael how to make tomato sauce while the guys plan revenge after the attempted murder of the Don.

1. Start by making the meatballs: Put all the ingredients except the olive oil into a large bowl. Use your hands to squish everything together and mix well.

2. Form the mixture into meatballs, about the size of golf balls. Use damp hands to make this easier. Set aside. You should have about 20 meatballs.

3. Pour enough olive oil into a wide pan to reach ½ inch up the sides. Heat on medium-high and cook the meatballs in batches, turning as they cook, until golden and just cooked through. Drain on paper towels.

4. For the sauce: Drain most of the olive oil from the pan and add the sausages. Brown all over and set aside with the meatballs.

5. Heat a little olive oil in a large heavy pot. Add the onion and cook over medium-high heat until soft, then add the garlic and cook for another minute. Pour in the canned tomatoes and tomato paste and stir to combine. Bring to a boil.

Continued on page 64 . . .

SERVES 6.

MEATBALLS
4 ounces ground pork
4 ounces ground veal
¾ cup dried bread crumbs
2 tablespoons fresh basil leaves, finely chopped
2 tablespoons fresh parsley leaves, finely chopped
1 large garlic clove, peeled and minced
¼ cup Parmesan cheese, grated
½ tablespoon salt
½ cup Tomato Sauce (page 59 or store bought)
1 egg
Olive oil, for frying

SAUCE
1 pound fresh Italian sausages
Olive oil
1 onion, peeled and finely chopped
3 garlic cloves, peeled and finely sliced
Five 14½-ounce cans crushed tomatoes
2 tablespoons tomato paste
½ cup red wine
1 teaspoon sugar
Salt
6 fresh basil leaves
1 pound pasta
Parmesan cheese and chile flakes for garnishing

6. Add the sausages and meatballs, wine, sugar, and a good pinch of salt and carefully mix to combine, then bring to a boil. Reduce heat to medium-low and simmer for 20 minutes, stirring every now and then, being careful not to break up the meatballs. Add the basil leaves and cook for another 10 minutes or until sauce has thickened. Taste again and season as needed.

7. Remove the meat, cover, and keep warm.

8. Meanwhile, cook pasta in a large pot of boiling salted water until al dente. Drain, return to the pot it was cooked in, add a generous amount of sauce, and toss to coat.

9. Serve each person a bowl of pasta topped with more sauce. Serve the meat alongside for everyone to help themselves. Make sure there are Parmesan cheese and chile flakes on the table for those who like them, and plenty of crusty bread to wipe up the sauce at the bottom of the bowl.

10. Any leftover sauce can be kept in the fridge for up to a week for a quick meal.

Pork and Veal Ravioli

Making homemade ravioli might take a little time, but they are so worth it. Usually made for special occasions, a christening, engagement, or a special birthday, a bowl of homemade ravioli is Mamma's love on a plate. Food traditions in Italian families are just as much about making the food as eating it. Many hands make light work, and making a big batch of ravioli with your family makes them even more special. Double or triple this recipe depending on how many you need to feed.

1. Roll out the pasta dough using a pasta machine (see page 56) to the second- or third-last setting (they should be almost see-through) and place on a lightly floured work surface. Cut in half lengthwise.

2. Place teaspoon-size mounds of raw meatball mixture along one sheet of dough, about 1 inch apart. Use a pastry brush to dampen the edges around the filling with a little water, then lay another sheet of dough over the top. Use your thumbs to press around the filling to seal and stick the dough together. Then use a pastry wheel or a knife to cut out the ravioli squares.

3. Lay the ravioli onto a tray lined with parchment, in single layers, as you continue to use all the dough. The ravioli can be placed in the freezer at this stage. Once frozen, transfer to an airtight container or snap lock bags and freeze for up to 3 months. When ready to cook, no need to defrost, just cook from frozen.

4. Cook the ravioli in a large pot of boiling salted water for 3 to 5 minutes, or until filling is cooked through. The easiest way to know when they're ready is to take one out and cut through to check.

5. Once cooked, drain and toss with your favorite sauce. Ravioli are delicious with a simple Tomato Sauce (page 59) or try with Bolognese Sauce (page 61) or Clemenza's Sauce (page 63).

SERVES 4 TO 6.

1 quantity Fresh Pasta Dough (page 56)
1 quantity Meatball mixture (page 63)
Flour, for dusting

Strozzapreti (Priest Stranglers) Pasta

I'm sure this pasta would have come in handy when Michael was dealing with the corrupt archbishop in *The Godfather Part III*. This is a simple, traditional pasta shape, quite hearty and thick (thick enough to strangle a priest apparently), and it goes really well with a rich sauce like Clemenza's Sauce (page 63), a simple Tomato Sauce (page 59), or try it with the Beef Braciole (page 137).

1. Roll out the pasta dough using a pasta machine (see page 56) to the fourth last setting. You don't want these too thin. Lay onto a lightly floured surface and use a knife or a pastry cutter to cut into strips about ⅓ inch wide. Dust with a little more flour and cut each strip about 4 inches long. Don't go getting a ruler out—this is a rough size, you don't need to be precise; this is rustic! Roll each piece with the palms of your hands to make long twist shapes.

2. Cook the strozzapreti in boiling salted water until al dente, about 4 minutes. They're thick, so they will take a while. The best way to check if they are cooked is to take one out and bite in. Once cooked, drain and toss with sauce.

SERVES 4 TO 6.

1 quantity Fresh Pasta Dough (page 56)

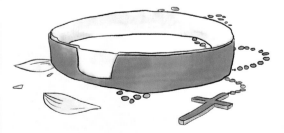

Gnocchi

Is there anything sexier than an Italian man making gnocchi? Cut to *The Godfather Part III* when Mary goes to visit Vincent at his club. The chemistry between them has been reaching a boiling point, and we all know where this is going. The clincher? Making gnocchi—the gentle hands caressing and forming the dough, turning it in the flour, a little nudge here, a little roll there, hand on hand, and next minute all that pent-up passion unfolds.

1. Put the potatoes, skin on, into a large pot and cover with water. Bring to a boil and cook until very tender. Drain.

2. When the potatoes are just cool enough to handle, peel and put them through a ricer. If you don't own a ricer, push the potatoes through a sieve. Do not use a potato masher as you won't get the same light and airy result. Spread out onto a board or your kitchen bench and allow to cool.

3. Sprinkle with the flour and use your hands to combine and form a dough. Knead briefly until smooth. Cover the dough with plastic wrap or a tea towel to prevent it from drying out.

4. Dust your work surface with a little flour, and working with one small chunk of dough at a time (keeping the rest covered), roll the dough into thin logs, about ¾ inch thick, then cut crosswise at 1¾- to 2-inch intervals. You can use a fork to add grooves to the gnocchi, or simply use your finger to turn them, leaving an indentation on one side (this is the way Vincent shows Mary how to make them), or simply leave them as they are, like little pillows, it's up to you. Place the gnocchi on a parchment-lined tray in single layers as you go.

5. You can now freeze the gnocchi on the tray until hard, then transfer into an airtight container or snap lock bags, and store for up to 3 months. No need to defrost, just cook from frozen.

6. Bring a large pot of water to a boil and add a good pinch of salt. Drop the gnocchi into the pot and stir gently. Once the gnocchi rise to the surface, they are ready. Remove with a slotted spoon and toss with sauce. Gnocchi are versatile and go with any sauce recipe in this book, but a simple tomato sauce is all they need.

SERVES 4 TO 6.

2 pounds starchy potatoes
4 cups all-purpose flour, plus extra for dusting

Clam Linguine

Just like when Michael was sent to assassinate Sollozzo and McCluskey, this recipe is all about timing. You need to have everything meticulously prepared ahead of time. Once you start, there's no going back. Don't panic, make your move at the right time, keep your eyes open, follow the instructions, and don't deviate from the plan. The planning has been done for you, don't overthink it. Just be calm, watch everything closely. Wait, but be ready. The pasta should be al dente at the precise moment those clams are open, then *bam*! Toss everything together and take it straight to the table. But please, don't drop anything!

Note: Because different brands of pasta vary in cooking time, read the manufacturer's directions before starting this dish as its success relies on the pasta and clams being ready at the same time. The clams take roughly 3 minutes to cook, so keep this in mind as you decide when to start cooking the pasta.

1. Check all the clams to make sure they are all tightly closed. Discard any that are open.

2. Put a large pot of water on to boil. Add a good pinch of salt and tip in the linguine. Give it a stir, and let it cook while you concentrate on the clam sauce.

3. Splash a good glug of olive oil (about ¼ cup) into a large skillet that has a lid. Add the garlic and chiles and cook over high heat for a minute or so, until fragrant. Add the wine and clams and stir to combine. Cover with the lid so that the clams can cook and open, about 3 minutes.

4. In the meantime, keep an eye on the linguine, stirring every now and then.

5. Once all the clams are open (discard any that are not), season with a little salt and pepper and scatter the parsley leaves over. Drain the cooked linguine, reserving a cup of the cooking liquid, and add straight to the pan with the clams. Toss to combine, add about ¼ cup of the reserved cooking water and a splash of olive oil, and toss over the heat to combine and thicken (about 10 to 20 seconds). If the mixture appears dry, add a little more pasta water and olive oil.

6. Serve immediately.

SERVES 4.

2 pounds clams, cleaned
1 pound linguine
Salt
Olive oil
4 cloves garlic, peeled and finely chopped
2 small red chiles, seeded and finely sliced
¾ cup white wine
Freshly ground black pepper
Handful of fresh parsley leaves, finely chopped

Pasta alla Sonny

This pasta apologizes to no one. With all the personality of Santino Corleone, this dish is traditionally known as *pasta arrabiata*, or "angry pasta." It's hot, fiery, and exploding with flavor that's like a whack in the mouth. If you can't handle the heat, adjust the amount of dried chile flakes.

1. Heat the olive oil in a skillet over medium-high heat. Add the onion and cook, stirring, until translucent. Add the garlic cloves and cook for another minute or so, until soft and fragrant.

2. Pour in the tomatoes, a pinch of salt, chile flakes, oregano, and basil and stir to combine. Increase heat and bring to a boil.

3. Reduce heat to medium-low and simmer, uncovered, for 30 minutes, or until sauce has thickened.

4. Meanwhile, bring a large pot of water to a boil. Add a generous pinch of salt and the pasta. Stir to combine. Cook until al dente, and then drain in a colander. Tip the drained pasta back into the pot and add a few ladlefuls of sauce. Toss to combine.

5. Serve with extra sauce, Parmesan cheese, and more chile flakes for the tough guys at the table.

SERVES 4.

Olive oil

½ onion, peeled and finely sliced

3 garlic cloves, peeled and finely sliced

Four 14½-ounce cans crushed tomatoes

Salt

2 to 3 teaspoons dried chile flakes

1 teaspoon dried oregano

6 fresh basil leaves

1 pound pasta

Bucatini Amatriciana

Bucatini Amatriciana is an iconic Italian-American meal. The star is the pork, which adds richness, salt, and powerful flavor to the dish. Bucatini is a type of pasta that looks like spaghetti but thicker and has a hole running down the middle. It is perfect with this robust sauce. This is a hearty dish full of flavor the whole family will love. Maybe when Clemenza didn't have enough time to make his famous sauce he could have thrown this together for the guys?

1. Splash some olive oil into a medium-sized skillet and heat on medium. Add the guanciale, pancetta, or bacon and cook, stirring, until golden and crisp. Add the onion and cook until tender. Add the chile flakes, oregano, a good sprinkle of black pepper, and the garlic and cook for another minute or so, or until the garlic is just beginning to color.

2. Pour in the tomatoes, add a pinch of salt, and bring to a boil. Reduce heat and simmer, uncovered, for 15 to 20 minutes, or until the sauce has thickened.

3. When the sauce is almost ready, bring a large pot of salted water to a boil. Add the bucatini, give it a stir, then cook, stirring every now and then, until al dente.

4. Drain the bucatini, reserving ¼ cup of cooking water, and immediately add a little of the reserved cooking water if the sauce seems dry. Toss to combine and cook until the sauce is thick and coats the pasta. Add the Parmesan cheese and stir through.

5. Serve with extra grated Parmesan cheese and chile flakes.

SERVES 4.

Olive oil

5 ounces guanciale, pancetta, or streaky bacon, chopped

1 onion, peeled and finely chopped

½ teaspoon dried chile flakes

½ teaspoon dried oregano

Freshly ground black pepper

2 cloves of garlic, peeled and finely chopped

Three 14½-ounce cans crushed tomatoes

Salt

1 pound bucatini pasta

¼ cup Parmesan cheese, grated

Shrimp Fra Diavolo

This is something Kay and Michael may have ordered when they ate their last meal together in the restaurant before Michael had to leave for Sicily. It is iconic Italian-American, but not something usually made at home. Often made with lobster, it isn't really an Italian recipe, rather an Italian-American creation. But who cares? It's delicious! Don't wait to go to a restaurant to order this; it's really simple to make at home and is a great meal for when you're feeling like something a little fancy.

1. Splash a little olive oil into a large skillet and heat on medium-high. Add the shrimp, in batches, cooking each side for about 1 minute, or until just cooked. Remove and set aside.

2. Add ¼ cup olive oil to the skillet and cook the anchovies over medium heat for 1 minute, stirring as they melt and disintegrate into the oil. Add the garlic and chile flakes and cook for another minute, or until the garlic is just starting to color. Pour in the wine and allow to bubble for a minute, stirring the pan. Add the tomatoes and a pinch of salt, and bring to a boil. Reduce heat and simmer for 15 minutes.

3. When the sauce is almost ready, cook the pasta in a pot of boiling salted water. Drain, reserving ¼ cup of the cooking liquid.

4. Tip the pasta into the skillet with the sauce and toss to combine. Add the cooked shrimp and the parsley and toss over low-medium heat to warm the shrimp through. If the mixture is dry, add a little cooking water and toss over the heat for a few seconds.

5. Drizzle with a little olive oil and serve with extra dried chile flakes for those who want more heat.

SERVES 4.

Olive oil

1 pound shrimp, peeled and deveined

2 anchovy fillets, packed in oil

4 cloves garlic, peeled and finely chopped

1 teaspoon red chile flakes

½ cup white wine

Two 14½-ounce cans crushed tomatoes

Salt

1 pound pasta

Handful of fresh parsley leaves, chopped

Pasta Puttanesca

Pasta puttanesca has a bit of a sordid history. Translated to "prostitute pasta," it was invented by prostitutes in Naples to lure customers in. I get the attraction—there's plenty of punch in the flavors, totally suited to satisfying a man's taste: salty, briny olives and capers, rich gutsy tomatoes, and spicy chile, that's enough flavor to tempt any man. Much more respectable than Lucy Mancini's approach to luring in a man: hitching up her bridesmaid dress and catching a quick moment with the bride's married brother. This pasta is rich, full of flavor, and best of all, quick and easy to make. Forget the name—this is perfect for the whole family!

1. Splash some olive oil into a skillet and add the chile, onion, and bell pepper. Cook over medium-high heat until the onion and bell pepper are tender, then add the garlic and cook another minute, stirring often.

2. Pour in the canned tomatoes and a pinch of salt and stir to combine. Bring to a boil, then reduce heat and simmer for 30 minutes.

3. When sauce is almost ready, cook the pasta in a pot of boiling salted water until al dente. Drain, reserving ¼ cup cooking water. Add the pasta to the skillet with the olives, capers, parsley, and a grinding of black pepper and toss to combine. Add a little cooking water if the mixture seems dry and toss again.

4. Serve with grated Parmesan.

SERVES 4.

Olive oil

1 red chile, seeded and finely chopped

1 onion, peeled and finely chopped

1 red bell pepper, seeded and finely chopped

4 cloves of garlic, peeled and finely chopped

Three 14½-ounce cans crushed tomatoes

Salt

1 pound pasta

3 tablespoons pitted black olives, chopped

1 tablespoon capers, drained and chopped

Handful of fresh parsley leaves, chopped

Freshly ground black pepper

Parmesan cheese for serving

Spaghetti with Olive Oil and Garlic

You get home late; there's nothing to eat. Aye, whaddya gonna do? You don't wanna get mixed up with ordering takeout. Do what an Italian would do. Just boil some spaghetti, toss it with some olive oil, anchovies, garlic, and chile, a little lemon and parsley, and badda bing—it'll blow your mind. Just make sure you don't drip any olive oil onto your nice Ivy League suit.

   Note: *Do not* leave out the anchovies, even if you think you don't like them. Trust me! Don't think of them as fish, think of them as a salty punch in the face.

1. Bring a large pot of water to a boil and add a generous pinch of salt. Add the spaghetti and stir. Cook until al dente.

2. While the spaghetti is cooking, pour the olive oil into a large skillet and add the anchovies. Cook on medium heat, stirring, until the anchovies melt and disintegrate into the oil. Add the garlic and chile and cook for another minute or so, until garlic is just starting to color (the spaghetti should be just cooked at this stage).

3. Drain the spaghetti, reserving ¼ cup of the cooking water. Tip the spaghetti directly into the skillet, add the lemon rind and parsley, and toss everything to combine. If mixture is dry, add the pasta water and a splash of olive oil. Toss over the heat for a few seconds to thicken the sauce and serve immediately with grated Parmesan.

SERVES 4.

Salt

1 pound spaghetti

¾ cup olive oil, plus extra if needed

3 anchovy fillets, packed in oil

4 garlic cloves, peeled and finely sliced

1 fresh chile, seeded and finely chopped

Finely grated rind of 1 small lemon

Handful of fresh parsley leaves, finely chopped

Parmesan cheese, grated, for serving

Fettuccine Alfredo

Ah poor Fredo. He was the kind one, warm, sensitive, sincere. He wasn't spicy and fiery like the others, he wasn't calculating. He was simply Fredo. Like a big hug of comfort, eager to please—just like this dish. Full of cream and cheese, it warms your soul and makes you feel better after eating it, even though it looks so simple on the plate.

1. Cook the fettuccine in a pot of boiling salted water until al dente.

2. While the fettuccine is cooking, put the cream and butter into a large skillet and heat on medium, stirring, until the butter is just melted. Do not bring to a boil.

3. Drain the pasta, reserving ¼ cup of the cooking water. Toss the fettuccine straight into the skillet, add the Parmesan cheese and reserved cooking water, and stir everything over medium-low heat until sauce is thick and is clinging to the fettuccine, about 30 seconds to 1 minute.

4. Season with a little salt and black pepper and serve immediately with extra Parmesan cheese if desired.

SERVES 4.

1 pound fettuccine
Salt
2½ cups heavy or whipping cream
½ stick of butter, chopped
1 cup Parmesan cheese, grated, plus extra for serving
Freshly ground black pepper

Orecchiette with Broccoli and Sausage

Sicilians are hardcore. Insult me? I'll bite your ear off! Hotshot Vincent Mancini clearly showed his ethnic roots when he took a chunk out of Joey Zasa's ear. "Temper like his father," sighs Michael. It's good to see Sonny's sordid affair with Lucy Mancini ended with this fine specimen who goes on to take over the family. But please, find some dignity. Just eat a plate of orecchiette (little ears) instead.

Note: You can replace the broccoli florets with broccoli rabe or other sturdy greens such as spinach or kale if you like. No need to add to the pot with the pasta, just add straight to the skillet once the sausage meat has browned and cook until wilted before adding the cooked pasta.

1. Add a good splash of olive oil to a skillet and heat on medium-high. Add the sausage meat and cook, mashing the meat up with the back of the spoon as you do, until browned.

2. Meanwhile, bring a large pot of water to a boil. Add a good pinch of salt and the orecchiette. Stir, then cook until the pasta is almost al dente. Add the broccoli florets to the pot with the orecchiette and continue cooking for another minute, or until pasta is cooked and broccoli is just tender. Drain, reserving ¼ cup of the cooking water.

3. Add another splash of olive oil to the skillet with the sausage meat and tip in the cooked orecchiette and broccoli. Add the garlic and chile flakes and cook, stirring, for 1 minute over medium-high heat, adding a little reserved cooking water if the mixture seems dry.

4. Add another splash of olive oil and toss through before serving.

5. Serve with grated Parmesan cheese.

SERVES 4.

Olive oil
1 pound Italian sausage, casings removed
Salt
1 pound orecchiette pasta
3 cups broccoli florets
Freshly ground black pepper
2 cloves of garlic, peeled and finely chopped
½ teaspoon dried chile flakes
Parmesan cheese for serving

Pasta alla Norma

Eggplants are as Sicilian as Vito Corleone and are used in many traditional dishes. You may be wondering why it is called "alla Norma." This dish originated from Catania, in Sicily, and was named after the opera *Norma* by the Sicilian composer Vincenzo Bellini. Ricotta salata is the traditional accompaniment, as it is creamy and salty at the same time, but feel free to use Parmesan instead.

1. Chop the eggplants, skin on, into roughly 1-inch chunks. Place in a colander and sprinkle with about 1 tablespoon salt and allow to sit for half an hour to remove excess moisture. Drain the liquid and pat dry with paper towels. Set aside.

2. Heat a good glug (⅓ cup or so) of olive oil in a skillet. Fry the eggplant in batches, in single layers so as not to crowd the pan, until browned. If the skillet becomes dry, add a little more olive oil as you go. Drain on paper towels.

3. Splash a little more olive oil into the pan and add the celery and onion. Cook over medium-high heat until soft. Add the garlic and cook until it starts to color. Add the tomato paste and cook, stirring for 1 minute, then add the cans of tomatoes, oregano, and basil. Stir to combine, bring to a boil, then reduce heat and simmer for 15 to 20 minutes, or until sauce has thickened.

4. Bring a large pot of water to a boil. Add a good pinch of salt and the pasta and cook until al dente.

5. While the pasta is cooking, add the fried eggplant to the sauce. Stir through.

6. Drain the pasta, reserving ¼ cup of the cooking water. Add the pasta to the skillet with the sauce and toss to combine. If the mixture is a little dry, add the cooking water and toss until thickened.

7. Serve with grated ricotta salata or Parmesan cheese.

SERVES 4.

2 eggplants

Salt

Olive oil

1 celery stalk, finely sliced

½ onion, peeled and finely sliced

4 cloves garlic, peeled and finely sliced

2 tablespoons tomato paste

Three 14½-ounce cans crushed tomatoes

½ teaspoon dried oregano

6 fresh basil leaves

1 pound pasta

Ricotta salata or Parmesan cheese for serving

Pasta alla Vodka

When Sonny is shot dead, it is left to Tom to give the bad news to the Don. But how do you tell someone you love that their son has been murdered? In a darkened room Tom tries to compose himself before going upstairs, but the Don, sensing something is wrong, confronts him before he gets a chance. "My wife is crying upstairs. I can hear cars coming to the house. Consiglieri of mine, I think you should tell your Don what everyone seems to know." To which Tom replies: "I didn't tell Mamma anything. I was about to come up and wake you just now and tell you." The Don notices Tom is having a drink; "But you needed a drink first." The stiff drink somehow dilutes the harshness of what Tom had to say. Just like in this classic Italian-American dish, the vodka somehow sweetens the sauce and cuts through the cream. It's only a small amount, but it has a powerful effect.

"Well, now you've had your drink."

"They shot Sonny on the causeway. He's dead."

If you don't feel a lump in your throat in this emotional scene, are you even human?

1. Heat a good splash of olive oil in a large skillet. Add the pancetta or bacon and cook over medium heat until golden and almost crisp. Add the onion and continue cooking, stirring often, until tender. Add the garlic and cook for another minute, until just starting to color.

2. Pour in the vodka and cook for 1 minute, scraping up any browned bits that have stuck to the bottom of the pan with a wooden spoon.

3. Add the tomatoes with a pinch of salt and stir everything together. Bring to a boil, then reduce the heat, cover, and let simmer for 10 minutes. Remove the lid and continue to simmer for another 5 minutes. Stir in the cream and basil, season with salt and pepper, and simmer for another 5 minutes (do not boil).

4. Meanwhile, cook the pasta in a large pot of boiling salted water. Drain, reserving ¼ cup of the cooking water. Add the pasta to the skillet, increase heat to moderate, and cook, stirring to coat the pasta, for 1 minute. Add a little cooking water if mixture seems dry.

5. Serve with grated Parmesan cheese.

SERVES 4.

Olive oil

8 ounces pancetta or bacon, finely sliced

½ onion, peeled and finely chopped

3 garlic cloves, peeled and finely sliced

½ cup vodka

Two 14½-ounce cans crushed tomatoes

Salt

1 cup heavy or whipping cream

Small handful of fresh basil leaves

Freshly ground black pepper

1 pound pasta

Parmesan cheese for serving

Meat Lasagna

No Italian celebration would be complete without a big dish of lasagna. It is the main meal served at Connie and Carlo's wedding. Imagine how many trays of lasagna would have been made to feed all those people! But that's the great thing about lasagna, you can make it in advance, so it's the perfect dish when you've got a lot of mouths to feed.

1. Preheat oven to 350°F. Add enough sauce to just coat the bottom of a baking dish about 10 by 12 inches and 4 inches deep. It doesn't matter if your dish is a slightly different size.

2. Lay the lasagna noodles in a single layer to cover the bottom of the dish. If they don't fit exactly, break them as needed. Don't worry, once cooked the lasagna sheets soften and mold together. Top with a few ladles of sauce. You want a nice even layer. Scatter with some of the grated mozzarella and Parmesan.

3. Keep layering the lasagna noodles, sauce, and cheeses until you reach the top of your baking dish. Top the last layer of lasagna sheets with sauce and the remaining cheese. Depending on the size of the dish you may not need all the sauce—store any leftovers in the fridge or freezer for another meal.

4. Pour about 1 cup of water around the sides of the assembled lasagna— you want to see the water coming halfway up the sides. This water is absorbed by the noodles as they cook and keeps the lasagna soft and moist.

5. Cover the top of the lasagna with a sheet of parchment (to keep the cheese from sticking to the foil) and then cover and seal with foil.

6. Bake covered for 40 minutes, then uncover and cook for another 15 minutes or until the cheese is golden and the lasagna noodles are cooked.

7. Allow to cool for 20 minutes before serving so that the layers can settle. This makes it easier to cut.

SERVES 8 TO 10.

1 quantity Bolognese Sauce (page 61), about 5 cups

Two 8-ounce boxes dried lasagna noodles

3 cups mozzarella cheese, grated

1 cup Parmesan cheese, grated

Baked Jumbo Shells

Like lasagna, baked jumbo shells are a great dish to serve a crowd. You can make it in advance and bake it in the oven when you need it. It's another classic Italian-American dish that is made to be shared with the whole family.

1. Splash a little olive oil into a medium-sized skillet and cook the sausage meat and onion, breaking the meat up with the back of the spoon as you do, until browned. Add the garlic and cook for 1 minute, stirring, then add the fennel seeds, chile flakes, oregano, a pinch of salt, and a grinding of pepper. Mix to combine, then set aside to cool completely.

2. Mix the ricotta with the egg, spinach, mozzarella, and half the Parmesan cheese. Add a little salt and pepper and stir to combine. Once the meat mixture is completely cool, mix this in. Set aside.

3. Bring a large pot of water to a boil. Add a good pinch of salt and the jumbo shells. Cook for 5 minutes, or until al dente, stirring every now and then so they don't stick together. Drain and toss with a drizzle of olive oil so the shells don't stick together.

4. Preheat oven to 350°F.

5. Spread about 2 cups of tomato sauce into the bottom of a baking dish. Stuff each shell with some ricotta filling and place into the baking dish, open side up in a single layer.

6. Spoon the remaining sauce around and on top of the shells, then scatter the remaining Parmesan cheese over.

7. Bake for 30 minutes or until cheese is golden.

SERVES 6.

Olive oil

8 ounces fresh Italian sausages, casings removed

½ onion, peeled and finely chopped

1 garlic clove, peeled and finely chopped

1 teaspoon ground fennel seeds

½ teaspoon dried chile flakes

½ teaspoon dried oregano

Salt

Freshly ground black pepper

16 ounces ricotta, drained

1 egg

2 cups cooked spinach, cooled, drained, and chopped

1 cup mozzarella cheese, grated

1 cup Parmesan cheese, grated

1 box (12 ounces) jumbo pasta shells

4 cups Tomato Sauce (page 59 or store bought)

Manicotti

After his family is murdered, Vito Andolini travels to the United States and arrives at Ellis Island. He is one of many immigrants looking for a better life in the United States, bringing with them their own traditions and cultures. One of the simplest ways to keep traditions alive and to stay connected with your homeland is through food. This is how America was introduced to the many diverse cuisines we enjoy today. Those cuisines influenced our own cooking, and new recipes emerged, like this recipe for manicotti, which is not traditionally Italian. You won't find it anywhere in Italy. The closest dish would be cannelloni, made with tubes of pasta. Manicotti are an Italian-American creation. Just as Vito Andolini was renamed Vito Corleone when he entered the United States, so too was this dish reborn with American roots.

You can buy a box of manicotti shells from the store to make these (then they would be more like the Italian cannelloni), but it is worth the effort to make the crepes. They melt in your mouth. Depending on how thin you make them, you may end up with more crepes than needed, but I always like to have a few spares in case any get broken as I assemble.

SERVES 4 TO 6.

6 eggs
Salt
1¼ cups all-purpose flour
1 cup water
1½ pounds ricotta, drained
1 egg, extra, lightly beaten
1½ cups mozzarella cheese, grated
1 cup Parmesan cheese, grated
Small handful of fresh basil leaves, finely chopped
4 cups Tomato Sauce (page 59 or store bought)

1. Start by making the crepes. Crack the 6 eggs into a large bowl with a good pinch of salt and whisk until thick and pale. You can do this with an electric mixer if you want. Add half the flour and whisk well to combine, then add the rest. Make sure to whisk well so the batter isn't lumpy. The batter needs to be nice and smooth. Pour in the water and whisk until smooth. Cover and set aside for one hour.

2. Heat a nonstick skillet over medium heat. Spray with a little nonstick cooking spray or add a little melted butter. Ladle in 2 to 3 tablespoons of the batter and tilt≈the skillet in a circular motion so that the batter runs and forms a thin circle. Cook for 15 seconds, then use a spatula to lift the crepe and quickly turn over to cook for 10 seconds on the other side, or until cooked (they don't take long). Set aside on kitchen towels in a single layer (don't stack them on top of each other or they will stick) while you make all the crepes.

3. Mix the ricotta, extra egg, mozzarella, ½ cup of the Parmesan, and basil together in a bowl. Season with salt.

4. Preheat the oven to 350°F.

5. Cover the base of a baking dish with about 2 cups of the tomato sauce.

6. Spoon roughly 2 to 3 tablespoons of filling down the center of each crepe. Roll the crepes around the filling into a log shape and place them into the baking dish on top of the sauce, seam side down. Spoon over the remaining sauce and sprinkle with the remaining Parmesan.

7. Bake, uncovered, until the cheese is golden, and sauce is bubbling—about 40 minutes. Remove from the oven and allow to sit for 10 minutes before serving.

Baked Ziti

The word "ziti" refers to a maiden, fiancée, or young bride. This recipe is literally "macaroni of the bride" and is a common dish served at southern Italian wedding banquets, such as Michael's wedding in Sicily. Apollonia was the most beautiful bride. Her beauty, her innocence, and her purity hit Michael like a thunderbolt. Their wedding dance is one of the most touching scenes in the movies.

There are so many variations of this recipe, and every Italian housewife would make it slightly differently. Some add chopped boiled eggs, marinated vegetables or olives, or homemade meatballs. This is a big bowl of comfort food, there's no formality here, just good old southern Italian hospitality that says, "Welcome to the family."

1. Preheat oven to 350°F.

2. Splash a little olive oil into a large skillet and add the onion and bell pepper. Cook over medium-high heat, stirring often, until tender. Add the pancetta or bacon and the sausage meat. Cook, breaking the sausage meat up with the back of a spoon, until browned. Add the garlic and oregano, a good pinch of salt, and a grinding of black pepper and stir to combine. Cook until garlic is fragrant, then remove from the heat and set aside.

3. Cook the ziti in a large pot of boiling salted water until al dente. Drain and return to the empty pot.

4. Add the contents in the skillet to the cooked pasta, as well as the cured meat, tomato sauce, and half the cheeses and stir well to combine.

5. Tip the pasta out into a large baking dish. Scatter over the remaining cheeses and bake for 30 minutes, or until cheese is golden.

SERVES 4 TO 6.

Olive oil

1 onion, peeled and diced

1 bell pepper, seeded and sliced

10 ounces pancetta or bacon, finely chopped

12 ounces fresh Italian sausages, casings removed

1 garlic clove, peeled and finely sliced

2 tablespoons dried oregano

Salt

Freshly ground black pepper

1 pound ziti pasta

7 ounces pepperoni, salami, mortadella, ham, or other cured meat, sliced

3 cups Tomato Sauce (page 59 or store bought)

1 cup Parmesan cheese, grated

2 cups mozzarella cheese, grated

MEAT, CHICKEN, and SEAFOOD

"Great men are not born great. They grow great."
–Vito Corleone

Italians don't eat a large amount of meat. When any kind of meat or seafood is on the table, it is generally backed up by many side dishes, so a little goes a long way. That's part of the reason why the Mediterranean diet is so healthy: a little of this, a little of that, and not too much of any one thing. Don't think of the meat, chicken, or seafood as the main meal, rather one small part of the meal. Don't be afraid to slice up single servings and put them out on plates to share so everyone can take a small piece. That way there's still plenty of room for bread, pasta, and side dishes. This is where Italian food becomes abundant and welcoming, with lots to offer and plenty to share.

Stuffed Oysters

Most Italian cooking is hearty and comforting, but for special occasions when you want to impress, like for the party held for Michael at the beginning of *The Godfather Part III*, you can't do better than a plate of oysters. Oysters are sophisticated, luxurious, and extravagant, just the kind of thing to serve when you've handed over a check to the Vatican for $100 million.

1. Preheat oven to 450°F.

2. If using fresh bread, pulse the bread in a food processor to form bread crumbs. Set aside.

3. Splash a little olive oil into a medium skillet and cook the bacon until crisp. Add the onion and cook until translucent, then add the garlic and cook until just starting to color. Add the bread crumbs, another drizzle of olive oil, and cook, stirring, until bread crumbs are lightly toasted, about 2 minutes. Remove from the heat and stir in the parsley, Parmesan cheese, lemon juice, and a little black pepper. Set aside and allow to cool to room temperature.

4. Place the oysters onto a baking sheet and distribute the bread crumb mix evenly over the tops. Drizzle with a little olive oil, then bake for 5 to 7 minutes, or until the oysters curl a little around the edges.

5. Serve immediately with lemon wedges.

MAKES 24.

2 slices of bread, or 1 cup fresh bread crumbs

Olive oil

2 slices of bacon, finely chopped

½ onion, peeled and finely chopped

2 cloves garlic, peeled and finely chopped

Small handful of fresh parsley leaves, finely chopped

¼ cup Parmesan cheese, grated

Juice from half a lemon

Freshly ground black pepper

24 oysters on the half shell

Lemon wedges for serving

Fried Calamari

When Johnny Fontane is having trouble with Jack Woltz, who won't let him star in his new movie, he turns to his godfather for help. As he sits on the edge of Vito Corleone's desk, head in his hands, he is as spineless as a squid. "I don't know what to do, I don't know what to do," he weeps. Vito Corleone jumps up, grabs him by the shoulders, and growls, "You can act like a man ... what's wrong with you?"

Being spineless is definitely not a characteristic the Corleone family will tolerate. But I'm sure they'd approve of these crispy calamari.

1. Cut down the length of the squid tubes and lay them out flat. With a sharp knife, score crisscross patterns all over the squid, without cutting all the way through. Now cut in half lengthwise and then crosswise, into strips, about ¼ inch thick. Set aside.

2. Put the corn starch, black pepper, chile flakes, garlic powder, and salt into a large snap lock bag. Add the squid to the bag and shake and squeeze until the squid is thoroughly coated. You can do this in a bowl if you like, but the bag method ensures a nice even coating.

3. Half fill a saucepan with oil or use a deep fryer if you have one. Heat to very hot, 400°F.

4. Remove the squid from the bag and shake off any excess flour. Cook in the hot oil, in small batches, for 1 to 1½ minutes, or until crisp and golden. Drain on paper towels and serve immediately with lemon wedges.

SERVES 4.

4 squid tubes, cleaned
¾ cup corn starch
1 tablespoon freshly ground black pepper
1 teaspoon ground dried chile flakes
½ teaspoon garlic powder
1 teaspoon salt
Oil, for frying
Lemon wedges for serving

Mussels Marinara

You may think of mussels as something you'd order at a restaurant. But they're actually simple to make at home as part of a family banquet. The most important thing is to make sure they're well cleaned before you cook them. There's nothing worse than eating sand with your mussels. Just imagine you're frisking someone: pull off the beard, scrub, rinse, then yell, "He's clean!" or say it in Italian, *E polito!*

1. Splash some olive oil into a large skillet and add the onion. Cook over medium heat until onion is soft, then add the garlic and cook, stirring, until fragrant.

2. Pour in the wine and cook, stirring, as it bubbles and reduces to half. Now add the tomatoes, oregano, a pinch of salt, and a grinding of black pepper and stir to combine. Add the mussels and bring to a boil. Cook over medium heat, stirring every now and then, for about 10 minutes by which time all the mussels should be open. Discard any that do not open.

3. Transfer the mussels to a large bowl and spoon as much sauce as you like over them to coat. Any extra sauce can be mopped up with bread or served with some pasta on the side.

4. Top with the fresh parsley and basil and serve.

SERVES 4 TO 6.

Olive oil

1 onion, peeled and finely chopped

3 cloves of garlic, peeled and finely sliced

1 cup white wine

Three 14½-ounce cans crushed tomatoes

1 tablespoon dried oregano

Salt

Freshly ground black pepper

4 pounds fresh mussels, scrubbed, de-bearded, and rinsed

Small handful of fresh parsley leaves

Small handful of fresh basil leaves

TIP: The golden rule of cooking mussels is that they should all be tightly closed when uncooked and open when cooked. Discard any uncooked mussels that are open (or won't close with a gentle tap) and any cooked mussels that remain closed.

Shrimp Scampi

This is a classic example of how an Italian-American dish was born. Immigrant Italian cooks had to adapt their recipes to use new American ingredients. This dish was originally made with scampi, or langoustines—small lobster-like crustaceans. Italian cooks swapped the scampi for shrimp, keeping the former name, and thereby creating the iconic shrimp scampi we all love today.

1. Heat a large skillet over medium-high heat and add the oil and butter. Cook until the butter melts into the oil. Add the garlic and cook, stirring, for one minute, or until fragrant. Add half the shrimp, a grinding of black pepper, and a pinch of salt. Cook, a minute each side, then remove to a plate. Repeat with the remaining shrimp.

2. Pour the wine into the skillet and let it bubble and reduce by half. Return the shrimp to the pan with the oregano and cook until firm and pink, about 3 minutes. Squeeze over the lemon juice and add the parsley leaves and bread crumbs and toss to combine.

3. Serve hot with bread to mop up the juices.

SERVES 4 TO 6.

½ cup olive oil

4 tablespoons butter

5 garlic cloves, peeled and minced

1½ pounds large shrimp, peeled and deveined

Freshly ground black pepper

Salt

1 cup white wine

1 teaspoon dried oregano

Juice of half a lemon

Handful of fresh parsley leaves, chopped

2 tablespoons dried bread crumbs

Sicilian Crumbed Fish

When Michael Corleone sees Apollonia for the first time, he falls immediately in love with her and wants to meet her desperately. But this is Sicily, and courting is much different than in other parts of the world. Permission must be granted by the father, and the whole family must get to know the suitor before the couple may plan to be married, which is the first time the couple can be alone together. Dating takes place over shared meals with extended family where food and wine bring people together to take part in the courting ritual. Heaping bowls of crumbed fish are served as we are drawn to the electricity forming across the table as Michael and Apollonia can't take their eyes off one another from opposite sides of the table.

1. Put the bread crumbs, Parmesan cheese, parsley, a good pinch of salt, and a grinding of black pepper into a medium-sized bowl. Mix to evenly combine. Put the flour into a separate bowl. Crack the eggs into a third bowl, add the water, and whisk to combine.

2. Dredge each piece of fish in the flour, shake off excess, then dip into the beaten eggs, then into the bread-crumb mixture, turning to coat evenly.

3. Pour olive oil into a skillet to reach a depth of about ¼ inch. Heat over medium heat, then add the crumbed fish in batches, cooking for about 2 minutes on each side or until the crumb is golden and the fish is cooked through. Don't let the oil get too hot or the crumb will burn before the fish is cooked. You want a nice steady bubbling of oil as the fish cooks.

4. Drain on paper towel and serve hot with lemon wedges.

SERVES 4.

2 cups dry bread crumbs
½ cup Parmesan cheese, grated
Small handful fresh parsley, finely chopped
Salt
Freshly ground black pepper
2 cups all-purpose flour
3 eggs
¼ cup water
4 firm white fish fillets, skin removed and cut into thick strips
Olive oil, for frying
Lemon wedges, to serve

Luca Brasi's Whole Roasted Fish

When Tessio walks in with a whole fish wrapped in newspaper, the boys know exactly what it means. They've been sent a Sicilian message, "Luca Brasi swims with the fishes."

There's no Sicilian meaning behind this roasted fish dish, and you can use any type of fish you like. Sea bass, bream, snapper, or similar fish will work well. Presenting a whole fish is very impressive and would be a great meal to serve for a special celebration with a selection of side dishes.

Allow about 1 pound of fish per person. You can cook one large fish or a few smaller ones, depending on how many people you have to feed and what you can get your hands on. The time required to cook will vary on the size of your fish. Keep an eye on it; once the eyes are completely white and the flesh is opaque and flaky, it's done.

1. Preheat the oven to 425°F. Line a large baking tray, big enough to hold the fish, with parchment.

2. Make three cuts crosswise across the fish that go almost all the way through to the center. Sprinkle some salt into the fish cavity and add a few sprigs of thyme, half the lemon slices, and a little bit of the garlic. Drizzle olive oil over the top of the fish and sprinkle liberally with salt. Stuff the rest of the thyme and garlic into the cuts made earlier and lay the remaining lemon slices over the top.

3. Roast for 25 to 30 minutes, or until the flesh is opaque. Test with a toothpick; the flesh should flake easily.

4. Serve with extra lemon wedges.

SERVES 6.

1 whole fish, cleaned and scaled, about 6½ pounds
Salt
Handful of fresh thyme
1 lemon, sliced
2 cloves of garlic, chopped
Olive oil

Chicken Cacciatore

When Vito Corleone comes home from the hospital, the family couldn't be happier. Everyone is there to welcome him home and Mamma is downstairs cooking up a big pot of chicken cacciatore for the family. It's the usual family table scene, happy chaos around the dinner table as everyone eats.

Cacciatore means "hunter" in Italian, and this dish is also known as "hunter's chicken," named because wives would make this dish for their men to eat while out hunting. It is symbolic that this is the dish Mamma Corleone cooks that night. Vito finds out it was Michael who killed Sollozzo and McCluskey, and his heartbreak is evident when he realizes his son, whom he never wanted to be involved in the family business, is now the hunted one.

SERVES 4.

Olive oil

3 pounds chicken thighs or legs, bone in

Salt

Freshly ground black pepper

4 ounces pancetta or bacon, diced

1 onion, peeled and sliced

1 carrot, peeled and diced

1 celery stalk, sliced

2 red bell peppers, seeded and sliced

1 red chile, seeded and sliced

2 cups brown mushrooms, sliced

4 garlic cloves, peeled and finely sliced

2 tablespoons fresh thyme

1 tablespoon dried oregano

2 tablespoons tomato paste

1½ cups red wine

One 14½-ounce can crushed tomatoes

24 ounces passata (pureed tomatoes, page 14)

Handful of fresh basil leaves

½ cup olives, pitted

Small handful of fresh parsley leaves

1. Heat a splash of olive oil in a large heavy pot and set to high heat. Season the chicken with a little salt and pepper and brown in batches. Remove and set aside.

2. Add a little more olive oil to the pot and add the pancetta or bacon. Cook, stirring, until almost crisp, then add the onion, carrot, celery, bell peppers, and chile. Turn heat to medium and cook, stirring every now and then, until vegetables have softened, then add the mushrooms and cook until everything is tender. Add the garlic, thyme, and oregano and cook another minute, or until garlic is fragrant.

Continued on page 116 . . .

3. Increase the heat and add the tomato paste and cook for a minute, stirring continuously, then pour in the wine. Stir, dislodging any browned bits that have stuck to the bottom of the pan, and let the wine bubble away for one minute or until reduced by half.

4. Return the chicken to the pot, add the tomatoes, passata, and basil and stir to combine. Add a good pinch of salt and a grinding of pepper, and keep stirring until almost boiling, then cover with a lid, reduce heat, and simmer for 30 minutes. The chicken should be almost submerged in the sauce. Add a little water if need be. Remove the lid and increase heat to medium and cook for another 10 to 15 minutes, or until sauce is thickened and chicken is cooked through.

5. Remove from heat, stir in the olives, and sprinkle with fresh parsley.

Chicken Piccata

"Piccata" means "annoyed" in Italian. I don't know why this chicken is annoyed, but hey, we all get a little annoyed sometimes, especially with our family. If something is bothering you, let it out—that's what the family is there for, to listen and help each other out. But keep it to the family. The Corleone family code is "don't let anyone outside the family know what you're thinking." This is a simple, delicious dish that's quick to make. It's perfect to serve on a big plate for the whole family to share with a simple green salad.

1. Cut the chicken in half lengthwise so you have 8 pieces. Season with a little salt and pepper. Put the flour and Parmesan cheese into a medium bowl and mix to combine. Dredge each piece of chicken in the flour mixture and set aside.

2. Heat a nonstick skillet over medium-high heat. Add ⅓ cup of the olive oil and 4 tablespoons of the butter. Once the butter has melted, add 4 pieces of chicken and brown well on each side, about 3 minutes per side. Remove and repeat with the remaining olive oil, another 4 tablespoons of butter, and the chicken. Remove and set aside while you make the sauce.

3. Pour the chicken stock into the skillet and add the lemon juice and capers. Bring to a boil, stirring. Add a pinch of salt and a grinding of pepper. Return all the chicken to the pan and turn to coat in the sauce. Reduce heat and simmer for 3 minutes, turning every now and then.

4. Remove the chicken from the pan and place on a serving platter. Add the remaining butter to the pan and use a whisk to incorporate into the sauce. Pour over the cooked chicken, sprinkle with the fresh parsley, and serve immediately.

SERVES 4.

4 chicken breast halves
Salt
Freshly ground black pepper
⅔ cup all-purpose flour
3 tablespoons Parmesan cheese, grated
⅔ cup olive oil
6 ounces butter
½ cup chicken stock (page 41 or store bought)
Juice of 2 lemons
3 tablespoons capers
Small handful of fresh parsley, chopped

Roast Chicken with Potatoes, Lemon, and Garlic

This simple dish of roast chicken will become your family favorite. This is Italian home cooking at its best, and there's not a tomato in sight. (But there is plenty of garlic!) This is the type of meal you bring to the table in its roasting pan and let everyone dive in. The potatoes will have absorbed all the chicken goodness, the onions will be soft and caramelized, and the chicken will be golden and crisp. The roasted lemon should be squeezed over the chicken at the table, bringing an earthy citrus flavor, and the garlic will be soft as butter inside its skin. Smear it over everything as you eat.

1. Preheat the oven to 350°F. Line a large roasting pan with a sheet of parchment.

2. Arrange the chicken in the roasting pan so the pieces fit snugly in a single layer. Nestle the onion wedges, potatoes, garlic cloves, and lemon wedges around the chicken. Drizzle generously with olive oil, about ⅓ cup.

3. Sprinkle with rosemary sprigs, oregano, a good grinding of pepper, and a generous seasoning of salt.

4. Cook for 50 to 60 minutes, basting with pan juices often, or until the chicken is golden and skin is crisp.

5. Serve at the table in the roasting dish.

SERVES 4.

3½ pounds chicken pieces (thighs and legs), bone in and skin on

2 onions, cut into wedges

3 large potatoes, cut into wedges

12 whole garlic cloves, unpeeled

2 lemons, cut into wedges

Olive oil

Handful of fresh rosemary sprigs

2 tablespoons dried oregano

Freshly ground black pepper

Salt

Family-Style Chicken Cutlets

The Corleone men may have been well prepared in every aspect of business, but Mamma Corleone's freezer would have been just as meticulously prepared with everything needed to cook up a feast any time of the day or night. That's Mamma's secret weapon.

Every Italian child will remember eating chicken cutlets. Italian housewives would buy a huge amount of chicken breast (or veal, which can be made exactly the same way), and spend a few hours turning them into chicken cutlets. Once made, they can be layered in between pieces of greaseproof paper and frozen for up to 3 months. That way you've got cutlets to pull out and cook up for the family in next to no time.

1. Cut the tenderloin off each chicken breast and then slice the breast into thin, roughly ½-inch-thick slices. The easiest way to do this is to slice on a slight diagonal from the top, cutting lengthwise, making each slice about 4½ inches long. There's no rule here—you can cut them as large or small as you like—just make sure they are all the same thickness.

2. Once you have sliced all the breasts, use a meat mallet to flatten all the slices and tenderloins to roughly ⅛-inch thickness. Set aside.

3. Put the flour into one medium-sized bowl. In another bowl, crack the eggs, add the water, and whisk to combine. Put the remaining ingredients, except for the olive oil, into a third bowl and stir to combine evenly.

4. Piece by piece, dredge the chicken into the flour, shake off excess, then dip into the egg, then into the crumb mixture, pressing to coat.

5. At this stage, the cutlets can be frozen in between layers of greaseproof paper for up to 3 months. Defrost prior to cooking.

6. Pour enough olive oil into a frying pan to reach ⅓ inch up the sides. Heat the oil on medium-high. Once the oil is hot, add a few cutlets at a time and fry gently. The oil should not be too hot, or the cutlets will burn on the outside before the chicken has cooked through. A gentle bubble around the edges is a good sign. Adjust heat as necessary. Cook on each side until golden, about 2 to 3 minutes per side. Remove to a paper-lined tray and repeat with the rest of the chicken.

SERVES 6 TO 8.

2 pounds skinless chicken breast fillets

3 cups all-purpose flour

5 eggs

½ cup water

3 cups dried bread crumbs

½ cup Parmesan cheese, grated

1 tablespoon dried oregano

Small handful of fresh parsley, finely chopped

1 tablespoon salt

Olive oil, for frying

Chicken Parmigiana

Chicken parmigiana is an iconic dish featured on almost every Italian restaurant menu in America. It is not a traditional Italian dish, rather another Italian-American creation inspired by the Sicilian dish eggplant parmigiana, where discs of eggplant are breaded and topped with sauce and cheese. Perhaps migrant restaurant owners, wanting to appeal to American customers who generally preferred meat dishes to vegetables, came up with the recipe to improve business. Because as we all know, you do what you gotta do for the family business.

You can substitute veal for the chicken if you like. Simply follow the recipe to make the Family-Style Chicken Cutlets (page 123), using thin slices of veal instead.

1. Pour enough olive oil into a frying pan to reach ⅓ inch up the sides. Fry the cutlets over medium heat, taking care the oil doesn't get too hot, for 2 minutes per side, or until crumb is golden and crisp. Drain on paper towels.

2. Preheat oven to 350°F.

3. Place the cutlets onto a parchment-lined baking sheet in a single layer. Spoon some tomato sauce over each one, then top with mozzarella and Parmesan. Sprinkle over the dried oregano.

4. Bake for 5 minutes, or until cheese is melted and bubbling. You can brown under a broiler if you like.

5. Spoon over any remaining warmed tomato sauce to serve.

SERVES 6 TO 8.

1 quantity Family-Style Chicken Cutlets (page 123)

Olive oil, for frying

3 cups Tomato Sauce (page 59 or store bought)

8 ounces mozzarella, grated

¼ cup Parmesan cheese

2 tablespoons dried oregano

Veal Marsala

Sitting down and sharing a meal with someone, breaking bread, so to speak, is a universal sign of trust. When Sollozzo and McCluskey chose Louis Restaurant to meet with Michael, it was meant to be a nice quiet meeting to talk some sense into the kid. They thought they had the upper hand. Michael was even frisked on the way in to ensure he wasn't concealing a weapon. Little did they know, as they sat down to a plate of antipasti and Veal Marsala ("the best in the city"), that Michael would shoot them both dead with a gun Clemenza had planted in the men's bathroom. As McCluskey's veal-filled fork flies through the air, Michael's destiny is changed forever. With the high-pitched scream of a train in the background, he turns and walks off, dropping the gun just like Clemenza told him to do. There was no turning back.

1. Heat 2 to 3 tablespoons olive oil in a skillet over high heat. When hot, add the mushrooms and cook, stirring often, for 5 minutes, or until the liquid from the mushrooms has evaporated and they start to brown. Add the garlic and cook for another minute, or until garlic is fragrant. Pour in the chicken stock and simmer for 3 minutes. Remove from the heat and keep warm.

2. Put the flour in a medium bowl. Pound the veal with a meat mallet to tenderize.

3. Heat 1 cup of olive oil in a large skillet over medium-high heat. When oil is hot, quickly dredge the veal in the flour, shaking off excess, and carefully lower into the pan. Cook, turning once, until brown—this should only take a minute per side. Remove and set aside on a platter. Cover lightly to keep warm. Increase heat to high and add the butter to the pan. Once melted, pour in the Marsala. Bring to a boil, stirring to scrape any brown bits from the bottom of the pan, until reduced by half.

4. Very briefly return the veal to the pan, add the mushrooms and parsley, season with salt and pepper, and quickly toss to coat.

5. Remove the veal to a platter and spoon the mushrooms and sauce over the veal.

SERVES 6.

1 cup plus 2 to 3 tablespoons olive oil

1 cup sliced mushrooms

1 garlic clove, peeled and finely sliced

½ cup chicken stock (page 41 or store bought)

1 cup all-purpose flour

1½ pounds veal cutlets

3 tablespoons butter

⅔ cup Marsala wine

3 tablespoons fresh parsley, finely chopped

Salt

Freshly ground black pepper

.LOUIS.
ITALIAN-AMERICAN
RESTAURANT
•THE BRONX, NEW YORK•

Veal Milanese

Veal Milanese is prepared in the same way as the Family-Style Chicken Cutlets (page 123), covered in bread crumbs laced with herbs and Parmesan. The main difference is the veal pieces are much larger than the chicken and are served on the bone. This is a man-sized meal fit to fill any tough guys.

1. Use a meat mallet to pound each veal chop to a thickness of about ¼ inch.

2. Put the flour into a wide bowl. In a second wide bowl, crack the eggs and whisk with the water. Put the bread crumbs, Parmesan, oregano, parsley, and salt into a third bowl, stirring to combine evenly.

3. Dredge each veal chop in the flour, then into the eggs, and then into the crumb mixture. Press to coat evenly.

4. Pour enough olive oil into a pan to reach ¼ inch up the sides and heat on medium-high heat. Cook the chops in batches until the crumb is golden and meat is cooked through—about 4 to 5 minutes per side. Fry gently and adjust the heat if necessary. If the oil gets too hot, the crumb will burn before the meat is done. Drain on paper towel and serve with vegetables or a simple green salad.

SERVES 4.

4 veal chops, bone in
2 cups all-purpose flour
4 eggs
¼ cup water
3 cups dried bread crumbs
¼ cup Parmesan cheese
1 tablespoon dried oregano
3 tablespoons fresh parsley leaves, finely chopped
1 teaspoon salt
Olive oil

Osso Buco

Osso Buco is a delicious, slow-cooked dish made with veal shin. "Osso buco" means "bone with a hole" and refers to the marrow hole in the center of the bone. It is melt-in-your-mouth delicious and perfect with a creamy bowl of Risotto Milanese (page 49). The meat takes up to 3 hours to cook, but don't be put off by that, some of the best things in life take time. Just like when Vito returns to Sicily as a successful man and finally avenges the death of his family by killing Don Ciccio—well worth the wait.

1. Heat a splash of olive oil in a large heavy pot on medium-high heat. Brown the osso buco shanks, seasoning with salt and pepper as you do, until golden all over. Remove and set aside.

2. Add a little more olive oil to the pan, then add the onion, carrots, and celery. Cook, stirring often, until tender. Add the garlic and cook for a minute, or until fragrant. Add the tomato paste and cook for another minute, stirring continuously.

3. Pour the wine into the pan and bring to a boil. Stir with a wooden spoon to dislodge any browned bits that may have stuck to the bottom of the pan. Now add the chicken stock, tomatoes, oregano, thyme, and a little salt and pepper. Stir to combine and bring to a boil.

4. Return the osso buco to the pot, turn to coat, and submerge in the liquid. The meat should be almost fully submerged—if not add a little extra stock. Reduce heat to low and put the lid on. Simmer for 2 to 2½ hours, or until meat is very tender. Remove lid and increase heat to medium and cook for another 10 to 15 minutes to reduce the sauce.

5. To make the gremolata: Mix all the ingredients together to combine evenly.

6. Serve osso buco with a sprinkle of gremolata.

SERVES 4.

OSSO BUCO

Olive oil

4 veal osso buco shanks (about 3½ pounds)

Salt

Freshly ground black pepper

1 onion, peeled and diced

2 carrots, peeled and diced

2 celery stalks, diced

4 garlic cloves, peeled and finely sliced

3 tablespoons tomato paste

1 cup white wine

1½ cups chicken stock (page 41 or store bought)

Two 14½-ounce cans crushed tomatoes

1 teaspoon dried oregano

4 sprigs thyme

GREMOLATA

Finely grated rind of 2 lemons

Handful of fresh parsley leaves, finely chopped

2 garlic cloves, peeled and minced

Salt

Sausages and Peppers

At Michael's son Anthony's first holy communion celebration, Frank Pentangeli, an old friend of the Corleone family, is getting hungry. It's a fancy event, and there are no trays of lasagna like we saw served at Connie's wedding.

Frank says, "Hey, Fredo, what's with the food around here? Kid comes up to me in a white jacket, gives me a Ritz cracker and some chopped liver, he says can o' peez. I said, eh, can o' peez my ass, that's a Ritz cracker and chopped liver . . . bring out the peppers and salsiccia."

Sausages and peppers are perfect comfort food. The only thing you need to go along with it is a good appetite and hunk of bread. Skip the crackers.

1. Splash a few tablespoons of olive oil into a large skillet over medium-high heat. Add the sausages and brown all over, remove from the heat, and cut into bite-sized pieces—about 1½ inches long. Don't worry if they have not cooked all the way through as they will be returned to the pan later.

2. Add the bell peppers and onions to the pan and cook, stirring often, until tender. Add the garlic and cook for another minute. Add the tomato paste and cook, stirring for one minute more.

3. Pour the tomatoes into the pan with a pinch of salt, a good grinding of black pepper, oregano, chile flakes, and the browned sausage and stir to combine. Bring to a boil, then lower heat to medium-low, add the basil, and cook, uncovered, for 5 minutes, or until sauce has thickened. Taste and season if necessary.

4. Serve with crusty bread or use to make Salsiccia Sandwiches (page 25).

SERVES 4.

Olive oil

1 pound fresh Italian sausages

1 green bell pepper, seeded and sliced

1 red bell pepper, seeded and sliced

2 onions, peeled and sliced

2 garlic cloves, peeled and minced

2 tablespoons tomato paste

One 14½-ounce can crushed tomatoes

Salt

Freshly ground black pepper

1 teaspoon dried oregano

¼ teaspoon dried chile flakes

Small handful of fresh basil leaves

Steak Pizzaiola

The traditional Sicilian version of steak pizzaiola uses beef shoulder. It's slow cooked, almost like a stew. In America, the dish has evolved, and uses a larger, leaner cut of steak. Either way, "steak cooked in the style of the pizza-maker," as it is loosely translated, is a delicious way to add a punch of Italian flavor to your favorite cut of steak.

1. Splash a little olive oil into a skillet and set to medium-high heat. Add the mushrooms and cook, stirring often, until they begin to soften. Add the onion and bell peppers and cook until tender. Add the garlic and cook for another minute.

2. Increase the heat, pour in the wine, and bring to a boil. Cook, stirring often, until wine has reduced by half, then add the tomatoes and oregano. Season with a little salt and pepper and bring to a boil. Reduce heat to medium and cook for 5 minutes, or until sauce is thick. Stir in the olives and set aside. Keep warm.

3. Heat a large skillet on high heat and add a splash of olive oil. When pan is very hot, cook your steaks to your liking. Depending on thickness and type of steak used, the time will vary. Once cooked, remove from the pan and set aside, lightly covered, to rest for a couple of minutes.

4. Serve steaks topped with pizzaiola sauce and a sprinkle of parsley.

SERVES 4.

Olive oil
1 cup mushrooms, sliced
1 onion, peeled and sliced
2 bell peppers, seeded and sliced
2 cloves of garlic, peeled and finely sliced
½ cup white wine
Two 14½-ounce cans crushed tomatoes
1 tablespoon dried oregano
Salt
Freshly ground black pepper
¼ cup black olives, sliced
4 steaks of your choice
Small handful of fresh parsley leaves, finely chopped

Beef Braciole

This is a hearty dish of thin slices of meat wrapped around a tasty filling served in a rich tomato sauce. There are many versions, but the addition of pine nuts and raisins is typically Sicilian. It's a little fiddly making the beef bundles, but just take your time. If you can perfect this traditional dish, you'll earn a lot of respect. You can buy thin slices of beef from the supermarket these days labeled as "braciole," or just use beef bottom round, slice it, and pound it thin.

1. Mix the garlic, bread crumbs, Parmesan, pine nuts, raisins, and parsley together in a small bowl. Add a little salt and pepper and drizzle with 2 tablespoons olive oil.

2. Pound the meat so that it's nice and thin and season with a little salt and pepper. Cut in half, about 4 inches long and 3 inches wide so you have 16 pieces. Don't get the ruler out, this is a rough guide and if your pieces are a little larger or smaller it won't matter. Cut the prosciutto slices in half and lay onto each slice of beef. Evenly distribute the bread crumb mixture over the top of each, leaving a border around the edges. Fold in the short edges, then roll the meat slice up to form a little bundle. Use toothpicks to hold together.

3. Heat a few tablespoons of olive oil in a large heavy pot and brown the braciole over medium-high heat in batches. Remove and set aside.

4. Add a little more olive oil to the pan and add the onion. Cook over medium heat until soft, then add the garlic and cook for a minute more. Pour in the wine and bring to a boil, stirring with a wooden spoon to scrape any browned bits from the bottom of the pan. Add the tomatoes, oregano, a little salt and pepper, and the browned braciole. Bring to a boil, then reduce heat to simmer. Turn the braciole to coat in the sauce and arrange them so they fit snugly, submerged in sauce. Add a little water if you need to. Cook for 1 hour nice and slow, or until meat is tender. Check every now and then and add water if the meat is not covered in sauce.

5. Increase heat to medium. Cook for another 10 to 15 minutes, or until sauce has thickened. Carefully lift the braciole from the sauce, remove toothpicks, and serve with sauce ladled over.

SERVES 4 TO 6.

4 cloves of garlic, peeled and minced

1 cup dried bread crumbs

½ cup Parmesan cheese, grated

2 tablespoons pine nuts

2 tablespoons raisins

Small handful of fresh parsley leaves, finely chopped

Salt

Freshly ground black pepper

Olive oil

8 very thin slices of beef, such as bottom round

8 thin slices prosciutto

1 onion, peeled and diced

2 garlic cloves, peeled and finely sliced

½ cup red wine

Two 14½-ounce cans crushed tomatoes

1 teaspoon dried oregano

SALADS and VEGETABLES

"I'm old school—I still believe in respect."
—Vito Corleone

You might think salads and vegetables take minor roles during a meal, but they provide a supporting role that makes the stars at the table stand out. Imagine *The Godfather* without Sonny. That's what the Italian table would be like without vegetables. Providing some kind of salad or vegetable at every meal is the Italian way, and the bonus is that it is a healthy and nutritious way to eat.

Don't think of salads and vegetables as bland or boring. Don't even think of them as light. These recipes are full of flavor and can stand alone in their own starring role any time. Serve them alongside any of the dishes from this book; there are no rules as to what goes with this or that. It's personal. It's your choice. Heck—serve them on their own with antipasti if you like! But please, don't skip this chapter—it'd be like watching the first and third Godfather movies and wondering what the hell you missed because you didn't watch *The Godfather Part II*.

Antipasto Salad

Italian's love antipasti, so it makes sense to turn it into a salad. It's the perfect accompaniment to almost any meal and was served with the Veal Marsala (page 127) when Michael assassinated McCluskey and Sollozzo at Louis Restaurant in the Bronx. There are many versions of antipasto salad, but generally they feature different kinds of preserved vegetables, salami, and cheese. Feel free to change and add anything you like depending on what you've got on hand.

1. Combine the lettuce, roasted red peppers, olives, salami, red onion, artichokes, provolone cheese, and tomatoes in a large bowl.

2. In a small bowl, combine the olive oil and oregano with ¼ cup of the reserved marinade from the jar of artichokes. Whisk together, then pour over the salad. Season with salt and pepper and mix everything together.

3. Toss the fresh basil over and serve.

SERVES 6.

1 head romaine lettuce, chopped

½ cup roasted red peppers, sliced

½ cup pitted olives, halved

1 cup chopped salami

1 red onion, peeled and finely sliced

1 cup marinated artichokes, drained and sliced, reserve marinade from the jar

4 ounces provolone cheese, cut into bite-sized cubes

12 cherry tomatoes

3 tablespoons extra-virgin olive oil

½ teaspoon dried oregano

Salt

Freshly ground black pepper

Handful of fresh basil, finely chopped

Caponata

Caponata is probably the most famous Sicilian vegetable dish, and every Sicilian housewife would have her own special recipe. Sometimes it has anchovies, or olives—this is a version that pays respect to the eggplant, the hero of the dish. Serve it on bread, tossed through pasta, alongside meat or seafood, or however you like. Caponata has a thousand uses. You can chop the vegetables smaller or larger depending on how chunky you like it.

1. Tip the eggplant into a colander and sprinkle evenly with a couple of tablespoons of salt. Allow to sit for 30 minutes as the salt draws out any moisture. Wipe off the salt and pat dry with paper towels. This removes any bitterness from the eggplant.

2. Heat the olive oil in a nonstick skillet on medium heat and add the bell pepper, celery, and onion. Cook, stirring often, until the vegetables start to soften, about 3 minutes, then add the eggplant and cook until tender, about 8 minutes. Add a little more olive oil if the pan seems dry. Take care not to squish the vegetables as you stir. Add the garlic, fennel seeds, and capers and cook for one more minute, or until garlic is fragrant.

3. Add the tomato paste, stir everything to coat, then add the vinegar. Bring to a boil and cook for a few minutes, stirring every now and then, until liquid is reduced by half. Pour in the tomatoes, sugar, a pinch of salt, and some black pepper. Bring to a boil then reduce heat to low-medium, and simmer, uncovered, until sauce has reduced and thickened, about 15 minutes.

4. Remove from heat, sprinkle with pine nuts and parsley, and serve.

SERVES 4.

1 eggplant, diced
Salt
⅓ cup olive oil
1 red bell pepper, seeded and diced
2 celery stalks, sliced
1 onion, peeled and chopped
2 garlic cloves, peeled and finely chopped
1 teaspoon fennel seeds, crushed
2 teaspoons capers, finely chopped
¼ cup tomato paste
⅓ cup red wine vinegar
One 14½-ounce can diced tomatoes
2 teaspoons sugar
Freshly ground black pepper
½ cup pine nuts, toasted
Handful of fresh parsley leaves, finely chopped

Green Salad

Michael Corleone learned many things from his father, from knowing how to spot a traitor to the notion of keeping your friends close and your enemies closer. He also learned the value of balance in life, with time for your family as well as time to ensure your business dealings complement one another. Michael knew the importance of keeping the balance and therefore loyalty of the other families in order to keep the peace.

Similarly, the most valuable lesson in Italian cooking is balance. Sure, there are plenty of hearty dishes and rich red sauces everyone loves, but you need to make sure there's something on the table that's a little lighter and fresher. If nothing else, a bowl of this simple salad will cut through any rich meal and keep everyone happy.

1. Put the lettuce, arugula, and cucumber into a large bowl. Drizzle with the olive oil and vinegar. Season with salt and toss to combine.

SERVES 4 TO 6.

1 small head of romaine lettuce, roughly chopped

1 cup baby arugula leaves

1 cucumber, peeled and sliced

¼ cup extra-virgin olive oil

3 tablespoons white wine vinegar

Salt

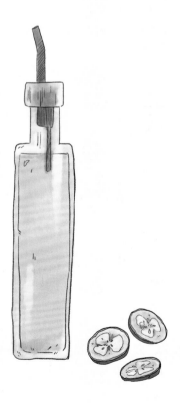

Caprese Salad

Growing your own vegetables can be incredibly satisfying. Tending to your own garden brings you back to nature, and your labors will be rewarded with incredible flavor ripened by the sun. This salad only has a few ingredients, so use the very best tomatoes you can find, ideally sun-ripened, fresh off the vine, bursting with flavor. If you don't have a beautiful tomato patch like Vito Corleone's, grab some from your local farmer's market.

1. Cut the tomatoes into roughly ¼-inch-thick slices. Cut the mozzarella into similarly sized slices. Arrange the tomatoes and mozzarella on a serving platter, overlapping. Sprinkle with salt and black pepper.

2. Scatter with basil leaves and drizzle a few tablespoons of olive oil over the top.

SERVES 4.

1½ pounds large ripe tomatoes
1 pound fresh mozzarella
Salt
Freshly ground black pepper
Large handful of fresh basil leaves, torn
Extra-virgin olive oil

Pepperonata

Pepperonata is a simple dish of stewed bell peppers. It is simple, but the sweetness of the peppers is perfectly balanced by a little sourness from the vinegar. Italians call this *agro dolce*, meaning sweet and sour. Pepperonata can be served warm but, just like revenge, this is a dish best served cold.

1. Put the onion, peppers, and olive oil into a medium-sized saucepan and cook over medium heat for 5 minutes, stirring often. Add a pinch of salt and the basil leaves. Stir to combine. Cook for another 15 minutes, stirring every now and then, until the vegetables are soft. Add the vinegar and oregano, stir to combine, and cook for one minute more.

2. Allow to cool before serving with fresh crusty bread. Leftover pepperonata can be kept in a sealed container in the fridge for up to one week.

SERVES 6.

1 onion, peeled and sliced

4 red bell peppers, seeded and cut into strips

¼ cup olive oil

Salt

Small handful of fresh basil leaves

2 tablespoons red wine vinegar

1 teaspoon dried oregano

Eggplant Parmigiana

Originally introduced into Sicily by the Arabs, eggplants became a staple ingredient for many of the most cherished Sicilian recipes, like this eggplant parmigiana. It wasn't always that way—eggplants were once feared because they were believed to cause insanity. This is how they got their Italian name—*melanzana*, which comes from the Latin term *malum insanum*, literally meaning "apple of insanity." Known for their bitterness, eggplants were to be treated with caution because they come from the poisonous nightshade family, and Sicilians knew all too well not to trust dangerous families.

1. Slice the eggplant crosswise into ¼-inch thick rounds. Place into a colander, sprinkling with salt as you layer them. Rest for 30 minutes to draw out excess moisture. Use a paper towel to wipe off the salt and pat dry.

2. Put the bread crumbs, oregano, and ¼ cup of the Parmesan cheese into a wide, shallow bowl. Mix to evenly combine. Crack the eggs into a separate bowl with the water and whisk well to combine. Put the flour into a third bowl.

3. Dredge each slice of eggplant in the flour, then egg mixture, then bread crumbs, pressing to evenly coat. Set aside.

4. Pour enough olive oil into a wide shallow pan to reach ¼ inch up the sides. Heat the oil over medium heat. Fry the crumbed eggplant slices gently in batches, turning once, until golden and crisp on each side. Drain on paper towels.

5. Preheat oven to 350°F.

6. Ladle some tomato sauce into a baking dish, roughly 9 by 13 inches, to just coat the bottom. Place eggplant slices over the top in a single layer, overlapping slightly. Now top the eggplant with another layer of sauce. Scatter a little grated mozzarella over the sauce and then some of the Parmesan cheese. Repeat until all the eggplant has been used—about 3 layers in total—finishing with sauce and a generous coating of cheeses.

7. Bake for 30 minutes, or until cheese is golden. Remove and allow to rest for 10 minutes for the layers to settle before serving.

SERVES 6.

2 large eggplants
Salt
2 cups dried bread crumbs
2 tablespoons dried oregano
1 cup Parmesan cheese, grated
5 eggs
½ cup water
1 cup all-purpose flour
Olive oil
3 cups Tomato Sauce (page 59 or store bought)
12 ounces mozzarella cheese, grated

Sicilian Fennel and Orange Salad

The scene in *The Godfather* when Vito Corleone dies while playing with his grandson in his tomato patch is one of the most touching yet dramatic scenes in the movie. Running around with orange segments in his mouth, he is no longer the calculating businessman, but a feeble, loving grandfather. The orange segments were never part of the script. Apparently, the little boy who played Vito's grandson was tired, and on a whim, Marlon Brando decided to put the orange segments in his mouth because it was something he had done with his own grandchildren. They shot the scene once, and the rest is history.

For this salad, just like that scene, it's the addition of the orange segments that makes all the difference. This is the perfect salad to eat with fish or chicken.

1. Trim the fennel, removing the thick outer layers, and reserve the fronds. Cut the bulb into quarters lengthwise, keeping the layers together. Slice as thinly as you can. Place into a serving bowl. Roughly chop the fronds and set aside.

2. Peel the oranges and cut away any pith. Slice into segments and remove the seeds. Add the segments and any juice to the fennel.

3. Add the sliced onion, olives, and arugula and toss to combine. Drizzle with the olive oil and lemon juice, add a good pinch of salt and a grinding of black pepper, and toss gently to combine.

4. Scatter with the chopped fennel fronds and parsley.

SERVES 4 TO 6.

2 medium bulbs of fennel

2 large oranges

½ red onion, peeled and finely sliced

½ cup pitted black olives

1 cup arugula

¼ cup extra-virgin olive oil

Juice of half a lemon

Salt

Freshly ground black pepper

Handful of fresh parsley leaves, finely chopped

Roast Rosemary Potatoes

The most important thing you need to know about cooking potatoes is to make sure you salt them well. This is not the time for a little girl's pinch, I'm talking a big, fat Clemenza-sized pinch, capiche? Otherwise they'll be as tasteless as wearing a leather jacket to a dinner party.

1. Preheat oven to 375°F. Line a large baking sheet with parchment paper and add the diced potatoes.

2. Pour the olive oil over the potatoes and add a good pinch of salt, some black pepper, and the rosemary and toss everything to combine.

3. Bake for 30 to 40 minutes, turning every now and then, or until potatoes are golden and crisp.

SERVES 4.

4 large potatoes, peeled and cut into roughly 1-inch cubes

¼ cup olive oil

Salt

Freshly ground black pepper

3 tablespoons fresh rosemary, finely chopped

Stuffed Mushrooms

Stuffed mushrooms are perfect for a fancy get-together. They seem fancy, but they're just mushrooms, after all. Just like the cotton that was stuffed into Marlon Brando's mouth while he was playing the Godfather, it's the stuffing that transforms the mushrooms into something truly memorable.

1. Preheat oven to 350°F. Line a large baking sheet with parchment paper.

2. Clean the mushrooms by wiping with a damp cloth. Remove the stems.

3. Mix ½ cup of the Parmesan cheese, bread crumbs, garlic, basil, oregano, ⅓ cup olive oil, a good pinch of salt, and a grinding of black pepper together in a small bowl. Spoon the mixture into the cavities of the mushrooms and place on the baking sheet in one layer. Drizzle the tops of the mushrooms with a little extra olive oil and sprinkle with the extra 2 tablespoons of Parmesan.

4. Bake the mushrooms for 15 to 20 minutes, or until tender and tops are golden. Serve hot.

MAKES 24.

24 medium-sized mushrooms (cremini or button)

½ cup plus 2 tablespoons Parmesan cheese, grated

½ cup bread crumbs

2 cloves garlic, finely minced

2 tablespoons fresh basil leaves, finely chopped

1 teaspoon dried oregano

⅓ cup olive oil, plus extra for drizzling

Salt

Freshly ground black pepper

Broccoli with Greens, Garlic, and Chile

You may struggle to get your family to eat a big bowl of greens, but this might change their minds. It's the magic of the olive oil, garlic, and chile that turns anything bland tasty. Just put it on the table confidently, and if anyone protests just say, "If you don't try this, you will disappoint me."

1. Cook broccoli in a pot of boiling water until just tender, about 30 seconds. Drain and refresh under cold water. Set aside to dry.

2. Heat the olive oil in a large skillet on medium-high heat and sauté the garlic and chile until fragrant, about 1 minute.

3. Add the greens and cook, stirring, until wilted.

4. Add the broccoli and a good pinch of salt and pepper, and toss for 30 seconds to combine. Drizzle with a little more olive oil if the mixture seems dry.

SERVES 4.

1 medium head of broccoli, cut into small florets

¼ cup olive oil

3 garlic cloves, peeled and finely sliced

1 large red chile, finely sliced

2 cups greens, trimmed and washed (kale, chard, spinach, or broccoli rabe)

Salt

Freshly ground black pepper

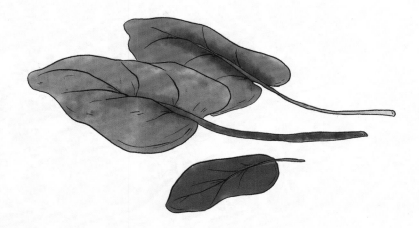

Stuffed Bell Peppers

There are so many versions of stuffed bell peppers from all over the world. The Spanish stuff them with cheese, the Greek stuff them with rice, the Lebanese stuff them with lamb, what's an Italian gonna do? Stuff them with meatballs of course! These are so good, you might want to double or triple the recipe.

1. Halve the bell peppers and discard the seeds and membranes. Fill the halved bell peppers with the meatball mixture.

2. Preheat oven to 350°F.

3. Add enough olive oil to a large skillet to reach ¼ inch up the sides. Set heat to medium. Cook the bell peppers, cut side down, for 2 minutes. Carefully turn over and cook skin side down for another 2 minutes.

4. Spoon a layer of tomato sauce into the bottom of a baking dish and place your bell peppers on top, cut side up. Spoon the rest of the sauce over and around the peppers. Sprinkle the tops with Parmesan cheese.

5. Bake for 30 minutes.

MAKES 6.

3 medium red bell peppers

1 quantity Meatball mixture (page 63)

Olive oil

2 cups Tomato Sauce (page 59 or store bought)

½ cup Parmesan cheese, finely shaved or grated

Spinach with Pangrattato

As Godfather, Vito had all the money he needed to give his family anything they wanted—a far cry from his humble beginnings back in Sicily. The poor needed to find ways to feed a family with next to nothing, and through necessity scraps were turned into delicious meals. Pangrattato is one of those creations. Meaning "grated bread," it was sprinkled over pasta to mimic the flavor of the more expensive Parmesan cheese. It also adds a lovely texture to cooked vegetables, such as this spinach dish.

1. To make the pangrattato: Tear up the bread and place into the bowl of a food processor with the garlic. Pulse until you have bread crumbs.

2. Heat the olive oil in a pan on medium heat. Add the crumb mixture and cook, stirring, until crumbs are golden. Remove from heat and set aside.

3. To make the spinach: Heat a few tablespoons of olive oil in a large skillet and sauté the garlic for one minute. Add the spinach and cook until wilted, stirring often. Add the lemon juice and season with salt and pepper. Toss to combine.

4. Remove from heat and sprinkle with pangrattato.

5. Any leftover pangrattato can be stored in a sealed container in the fridge.

SERVES 4.

PANGRATTATO
3 slices stale bread
1 large garlic clove, peeled and finely chopped
3 tablespoons olive oil

SPINACH
Olive oil
2 garlic cloves, peeled and finely sliced
1½ pounds spinach, rinsed, drained, and roughly chopped
Juice of half a lemon
Salt
Freshly ground black pepper

Risotto-Stuffed Tomatoes

There are a couple of rules every Italian mamma abides by when it comes to cooking: Always cook more than you need and never throw anything out. It's Mamma's worst nightmare to see all the dishes clean at the end of the meal—she'd be worried she didn't cook enough. Some leftover food means everyone was full and satisfied—that makes Mamma smile. Then she's got leftovers to turn into another meal, like these Risotto-Stuffed Tomatoes. They're so good, even if you don't have any leftover risotto hanging around, you can make a batch of Risotto Milanese (page 49) specially for it.

1. Preheat oven to 375°F. Line a baking dish with parchment.

2. Slice the tops off the tomatoes, about ½ inch from the top. Set aside. Scoop out the flesh and juice of the tomatoes (discard the flesh and juice, or set aside for something else), being careful not to cut through the base. Season inside the cavities with salt and pepper.

3. Mix the risotto with the cheeses, the beaten egg, and the basil. Spoon the mixture into the hollow tomatoes and then top with the slices you cut off earlier, so they look like little lids.

4. Drizzle the tops with a little olive oil and bake for 15 minutes, or until the skin of the tomatoes looks wrinkly and soft.

SERVES 4.

8 medium, round tomatoes
Salt
Freshly ground black pepper
2 cups cold risotto
3 tablespoons Parmesan cheese, grated
¼ cup mozzarella cheese, grated
1 egg, lightly beaten
6 fresh basil leaves, finely chopped
Olive oil

DESSERT

Italians are renowned for making beautiful desserts, but they don't really indulge in them too often. Traditionally, Italians would eat something sweet in the morning with coffee, something simple like a biscuit, and are more inclined to eat fruit at the end of an everyday meal. Most decadent desserts are made for special occasions, like birthdays, weddings, and baptisms, or special times of the year such as Easter, Christmas, or other religious festivities. But don't let that stop you from making these desserts whenever you like.

You only live once after all. Be like Clemenza when he takes his box of cannoli: Treat yourself after a job well done.

Fruit

You may think that Italians are always eating cream cake and cannoli. But in fact, desserts are most often reserved for special occasions. Traditionally, fruit is served after a meal. Something as simple as a perfectly ripe pear, like the one Vito gives his young wife in *The Godfather Part II*, can be a beautiful thing. Even at Connie's wedding, where there is that magnificent wedding cake, we see Tessio sitting at the table peeling an orange with a knife.

Buy whatever is in season and bring it to the table for your family at the end of every meal. If you buy good-quality produce, it'll be an offer they can't refuse.

Almond Cookies

Italian celebrations are big noisy affairs with lots of music and dancing and plenty of wine, champagne, and food, where the whole family is included. In the Godfather movies, the images of children laughing, sitting under tables playing, and dancing with adults, with their little feet on top of adult feet, as well as the older generation all dressed up and singing along to the music, is what family get-togethers are all about. These traditional almond cookies are commonly served at celebrations to go with coffee at the end of a feast and enjoyed by young and old alike. But you don't need to wait for a celebration; these are delicious (and very addictive) anytime.

1. Put the almond meal and sugar into the bowl of a food processor and pulse for 1 minute. Add the flour, baking powder, egg whites, vanilla, Amaretto or almond extract, and lemon rind and process until evenly combined. Cover and set aside for 30 minutes.

2. Preheat oven to 340°F. Line a large baking sheet with parchment.

3. Put the powdered sugar into a bowl. Roll the almond mixture into walnut-sized balls and flatten slightly. Roll in the powdered sugar to coat and place onto the baking sheet, leaving a little room between each one. Top with a blanched almond.

4. Bake for 15 to 20 minutes in the upper part of the oven. The cookies are ready when they are just starting to color.

5. Allow to cool completely.

MAKES 20.

7 ounces almond meal

1 cup superfine sugar

2 tablespoons all-purpose flour

1 teaspoon baking powder

2 egg whites, lightly beaten

½ teaspoon vanilla extract

2 tablespoons Amaretto liqueur (or ½ teaspoon almond extract)

Finely grated rind of half a lemon

2 cups powdered sugar

7 ounces blanched whole almonds

Aniseed Biscotti

Biscotti are one of the most well-known Italian cookies. Literally meaning "twice cooked" biscotti are first cooked as a large log, then sliced and cooked again to obtain that crisp texture they are known for. There are many different versions of biscotti; this one is flavored with ground anise seeds and the Italian liqueur Anisette, which gives them a delicious licorice flavor. Anisette is a popular Italian liqueur, usually drunk straight from a shot glass, and it appears in a few scenes in the Godfather movies, particularly when important discussions are taking place and a stiff drink is required.

1. Preheat oven to 350°F. Line a large baking sheet with parchment.

2. Put the flour, baking powder, sugar, salt, almonds, and ground anise seeds into a large bowl and mix well. Whisk the eggs, vanilla, and Anisette or anise extract together in another small bowl then add to the dry ingredients. Mix to combine. This is a stiff dough, so you will need to get your hands in there to squish it all together.

3. Shape the dough into two logs, about 8 to 10 inches long. Use damp hands to do this. Flatten the tops slightly and bake for 30 minutes. Remove and allow to cool on the baking sheet.

4. Reduce the oven temperature to 275°F.

5. Use a serrated knife to cut diagonally through the cooled logs, making ¼-inch-wide slices. Lay the slices cut side up onto the baking sheet and return to the oven for another 30 to 40 minutes, turning once halfway through cooking, or until the biscotti are dry and crisp.

6. Cool on wire racks.

MAKES 25.

2 cups all-purpose flour
1½ teaspoons baking powder
1 cup superfine sugar
Pinch of salt
1 cup whole almonds
1 tablespoon ground anise seeds
2 eggs
½ teaspoon vanilla extract
2 tablespoons Anisette liqueur or 2 teaspoons anise extract

Zabaglione

This creamy Marsala-spiked custard is as smooth as Johnny Fontane's voice. Serve warm with savoiardi biscuits (ladyfingers) or chill and serve with fresh berries.

1. Pour enough water into a small saucepan to reach ⅓ of the way up the sides. Bring to a boil then reduce the heat and keep on a low simmer.

2. Whisk the egg yolks and sugar together in a heatproof bowl until thick and pale. Add the Marsala and whisk to combine.

3. Sit the bowl on top of the saucepan with simmering water and whisk continuously until the mixture has tripled in volume—about 5 minutes. Ensure the water from the saucepan does not touch the bottom of the bowl or the eggs may curdle.

4. Spoon into glasses or bowls and serve.

SERVES 4.

5 egg yolks
⅔ cup superfine sugar
½ cup Marsala wine

Cannoli

"Leave the gun, take the cannoli."
—Clemenza

Cannoli are one of the most famous Italian pastries. Originating in Sicily, these crispy tubes of pastry stuffed with creamy sweet ricotta with candied fruit are simply to die for. No wonder Clemenza couldn't leave that box behind! You need cannoli forms to make these; they are cylindrical stainless steel tubes easily found in kitchenware stores.

You can dip the ends of your cannoli in melted chocolate and then in chopped pistachios, or simply dip the filled cannoli into the pistachios at the end, or leave them plain, the choice is yours.

1. To make the cannoli shells: Put the flour and butter into the bowl of a food processor and pulse until the mixture looks like bread crumbs. Add the sugar, salt, cinnamon, vanilla, wine, vinegar, and egg white (reserve yolk for later) and blend until the mixture forms a dough.

2. Squish the dough together into a ball with your hands and cover with plastic wrap. Let rest for 30 minutes.

3. Cut the dough into 4 pieces. You can roll it out with a rolling pin, but because it is a stiff dough it is easiest to run it through a pasta machine. Roll it out nice and thin, starting at the widest setting of the pasta machine, then run it through each setting until it's about 1⁄16 inch thick. If you find the dough is a little tacky, dust with a little flour as you go. Cut into rounds using a 4-inch round cookie cutter. Cover the dough rounds with a damp tea towel to prevent from drying out as you make the cannoli.

4. Grease your cannoli forms. Mix the reserved egg yolk with a couple of tablespoons of water.

5. Wrap each circle of dough around each cannoli form and dab a little of the egg yolk mixture on one edge to act as glue to join the edges together.

6. Half fill a saucepan with oil and heat until it reaches a temperature of 350°F. Carefully drop in a few cannoli at a time—they should bubble up straight away. Once they rise to the surface and are dark golden and blistered, remove with tongs and drain on paper towel. Cool a little, then use a tea towel to hold the cannoli and gently slide off the tube. Continue with remaining cannoli.

Continued on page 178 . . .

MAKES 32.

CANNOLI SHELLS
2 cups all-purpose flour
1 ounce cold butter, diced
2 tablespoons superfine sugar
1 pinch of salt
½ teaspoon ground cinnamon
½ teaspoon vanilla extract
3 tablespoons white wine
1 tablespoon white vinegar
1 egg, separated
Vegetable oil, for frying

RICOTTA FILLING
4 ounces whipping cream
1 pound fresh ricotta
1 tablespoon vanilla extract
1¾ cups powdered sugar, plus extra for serving
3 tablespoons mixed candied fruit peel, finely chopped

DECORATION
12 ounces dark chocolate, melted (optional)
Chopped pistachios for garnish (optional)

7. Cool cannoli shells completely before filling. Unfilled cannoli shells can be stored in an airtight container for one week, or frozen for up to 3 months. Dip in chocolate and pistachios (optional) and fill with the ricotta cream (method follows), as close to serving as possible so that the shells don't get soggy.

8. To make the ricotta cream: Beat the cream with an electric mixer until stiff peaks form. Set aside. In a separate bowl, beat the ricotta and vanilla with an electric mixer until smooth. Add the powdered sugar and beat well to combine. Fold in the candied peel and whipped cream. Spoon into a piping bag fitted with a ⅓-inch nozzle.

9. Dip the ends of the unfilled cannoli tubes into the melted chocolate and then in chopped pistachios if you like, and set aside to set before filling with ricotta cream. Alternatively, just fill with ricotta cream and dip the ends in chopped pistachios. Dust with powdered sugar to serve.

Angel Wings

Angels are a symbol of Christianity, purity, and faith. It is that sense of faith that is so compelling in Michael's powerful confession to Cardinal Lamberto in *The Godfather Part III*. In a truly memorable scene he confesses his sins, including having his brother Fredo killed. "I killed my mother's son. I killed my father's son," he weeps. To which this "true priest" says, "Your sins are terrible, and it is just that you suffer. Your life could be redeemed. But I know you don't believe that." Michael vows he will sin no more, but he is still hit with his greatest punishment of all, the brutal death of his own daughter. His scream of haunting anguish, as if all his sorrow and guilt have been condensed in that one moment, is heartbreaking to watch. In the end, when he dies an old man, did the angels come down and welcome him into heaven? Had he suffered enough to repent his sins?

These crispy ribbons of dough covered in powdered sugar resemble angels' wings and are also known as *crostoli*. They are light and airy and typically served at religious celebrations. They are so deliciously addictive it would be a sin not to make them.

1. Mix the flour, baking powder, salt, sugar, and lemon rind together in a large bowl. Whisk the egg, ¾ tablespoon of the vegetable oil, wine, vinegar, and vanilla together in a separate bowl. Make a well in the center of the dry mixture and pour in the wet mixture and mix well to combine.

2. Knead the dough on a lightly floured surface, or in an electric mixer fitted with a dough hook, until smooth. This is a stiff dough so if you are kneading by hand, it will require a bit of effort.

3. Wrap in plastic wrap and let rest for 30 minutes.

4. The easiest way to work with the dough is by using a pasta machine. You can roll it out with a rolling pin, but that will be much more difficult.

5. Cut the dough into 6 equal pieces. Work with one piece at a time, keeping the rest covered so they don't dry out. Roll the dough through the widest setting of your pasta machine, then fold in half and repeat 5 times. Now run the dough through each setting once, dusting with flour if it starts to stick, until the fifth or sixth setting. The sheet of dough will be almost see-through.

Continued on page 182 . . .

MAKES 40.

1⅔ cups all-purpose flour
½ teaspoon baking powder
¼ teaspoon salt
1 teaspoon sugar
Finely grated rind of half a lemon
1 egg
¾ tablespoon vegetable oil, plus extra for frying
2½ tablespoons white wine
1½ tablespoons white wine vinegar
1 teaspoon vanilla extract
Powdered sugar for dusting

6. Place the sheet of dough onto a lightly floured surface and use a fluted pastry wheel to cut roughly 3-inch lengths. Then make a lengthwise cut in the center of each piece, making sure you don't cut all the way to the ends. Fold one end of dough through the center cut and lay out flat. Set the angel wings aside on a tray in a single layer as you repeat with all the dough. You will need lots of room!

7. Pour enough vegetable oil into a large, wide pot, to reach halfway up the sides. Heat to 350°F, or until a small piece of dough sizzles immediately when dropped in the oil.

8. Fry the angel wings in small batches, turning once during cooking. They cook fast, only a few seconds, so keep an eye on them. When ready they will be golden and blistered. Remove and drain on paper towels.

9. Dust well with powdered sugar. Store for up to 1 month in an airtight container.

Olive Oil and Orange Cake

This cake contains the two ingredients most often featured in the Godfather movies: olive oil and oranges. Using olive oil in place of butter in a cake is quite common in Italy, but please don't use extra-virgin olive oil here as the flavor would be too strong.

The addition of the toasted almonds at the end not only makes this cake look beautiful but also gives a delicious nutty crunch. Feel free to omit them if desired and simply dust well with powdered sugar.

1. Preheat oven to 350°F. Grease and line the base of a 9-inch round spring-form pan with parchment.

2. Roughly chop the whole oranges (including the rind) and place into a food processor. Pulse until mixture is pureed. Add the olive oil and pulse until blended.

3. Mix the flour, almond meal, and baking powder in a large bowl. Add the orange puree and stir to combine.

4. In a separate bowl, beat the eggs with an electric mixer until light and fluffy. Add the sugar gradually, while still beating, until the sugar is all incorporated and the mixture is thick.

5. Add half the egg mixture to the orange and flour mixture and gently fold through. Repeat with the remaining egg mixture.

6. Pour the batter into the prepared cake pan and bake for 50 minutes, or until the cake is cooked through when tested with a skewer.

7. Let the cake cool for 10 minutes in the pan, then remove and set on a wire rack and sprinkle the top with the flaked almonds. Once cool, dust generously with powdered sugar before serving.

SERVES 8.

2 oranges
⅓ cup olive oil
1 cup all-purpose flour
1 cup almond meal
1½ teaspoons baking powder
4 eggs
1½ cups sugar
½ cup flaked almonds, toasted
Powdered sugar for dusting

Ricotta Crostata

A crostata is a traditional sweet Italian tart. They are often made with jam, fruit, or custard. This one uses creamy ricotta, like an Italian version of a cheesecake. Just the thing Enzo the baker would have whipped up in his bakery and delivered to Italian families for special occasions. Don't worry, you don't need to be a professional baker to make your own pastry—it's simpler to make than you think.

1. To make the pastry: Put the flour, powdered sugar, lemon rind, and salt into the bowl of a food processor and pulse to combine. Add the cold butter and pulse until the mixture resembles coarse bread crumbs. Add the eggs and vanilla extract and pulse again just until the mixture clings together to form a dough. If it is a little dry and not coming together, add a little cold water, a tablespoon at a time (no more than 2 tablespoons). Remove from the food processor and split the dough in two, ⅔ of the dough into one disk and the remaining ⅓ in another. Wrap in plastic wrap and refrigerate for at least 30 minutes.

2. If you want to make the dough by hand, combine the flour, sugar, lemon rind, and salt in a large bowl. Add the cold butter and use the tips of your fingers to rub and incorporate. Make a well in the center and add the eggs and vanilla, then knead quickly into a dough.

3. Once the dough has chilled, roll out the larger disk of pastry in between two sheets of parchment paper until it's about ⅛ inch thick. Peel one sheet of paper off and flip the pastry into a 9-inch loose bottom tart pan. Peel the other sheet off and press the pastry evenly into the pan. Trim the edges and place in the freezer to chill.

4. Add any pastry trimmings to the remaining pastry disk and roll in between two sheets of parchment paper to the same thickness. Peel the top sheet of paper off and place the dough on a large tray that will fit in your fridge. Cut the pastry into strips about ½ inch wide and refrigerate.

Continued on page 188 . . .

SERVES 8 TO 10.

PASTRY
2½ cups all-purpose flour
¼ cup powdered sugar
Finely grated rind of half a lemon
Pinch of salt
6 ounces cold butter, diced
1 egg
½ teaspoon vanilla extract

FILLING
⅓ cup sultanas
½ cup rum, brandy, or warm water
13 ounces ricotta, drained
⅓ cup superfine sugar
¼ cup heavy cream
1 teaspoon vanilla extract
Finely grated rind of 1 orange
Finely grated rind of 1 lemon
2 eggs
1 tablespoon milk
Powdered sugar, for dusting

5. Meanwhile, make the filling: Place the sultanas into a small bowl and pour over the alcohol or water. Set aside for 20 minutes. Preheat oven to 350°F.

6. Place the ricotta and sugar into a bowl and beat until smooth and well combined. Add the cream, vanilla, orange and lemon rind, and one egg and mix to combine. Drain the sultanas, discarding the liquid, and fold through the mixture.

7. Spoon the filling into the chilled pastry shell and smooth the top. Whisk one egg with 1 tablespoon milk in a small bowl; this is your egg wash.

8. Take the cut pastry strips out of the fridge and place them over the top of the ricotta mixture in a lattice pattern, brushing with a little egg wash to join the edges, cutting lengths to fit as needed. Brush all over with the remaining egg wash and bake for 40 to 45 minutes, or until pastry is golden and crisp.

9. Allow to cool completely before dusting with powdered sugar to serve.

Tiramisu

The iconic Italian dessert, tiramisu translates to "pick me up" referring to the hit of strong coffee you get in every bite. Just like a Sicilian being asked a favor at his daughter's wedding, you can't say no to tiramisu.

1. Pour some water into a small saucepan to reach about one-third of the way up the sides. Bring to a boil then reduce heat and simmer.

2. Put the yolks and sugar into a heatproof bowl and whisk until thick and pale. Place the bowl on top of the saucepan, still simmering, and whisk continuously until mixture triples in volume, about 5 minutes. Make sure the water does not touch the bottom of the bowl. Set aside to cool.

3. Beat the cream with an electric mixer until stiff peaks form. Fold the whipped cream, mascarpone, and vanilla into the cooled egg mixture and set aside.

4. Pour the coffee and Marsala into a shallow bowl. Dip the savoiardi biscuits into this mixture, one by one, and place into a roughly 8-by-12-inch dish that is at least 4 inches deep, in a single layer. Your dish doesn't need to be exactly 8 by 12 inches, close to this size will do. Cut the biscuits to fit as needed. You may need more or less depending on the size of your pan.

5. Spoon half the cream mixture over the top of the biscuit layer, then repeat with another layer of coffee-dipped savoiardi. Spoon the remaining cream mixture over the top, use a spatula to level the cream, and dust all over with the cocoa powder and drinking chocolate.

6. Cover with plastic wrap and refrigerate for at least 4 hours, or overnight.

SERVES 10.

6 egg yolks
1¼ cups superfine sugar
1¾ cups heavy or whipping cream
8 ounces mascarpone
1 teaspoon vanilla extract
1 cup brewed strong black coffee, cooled
3 tablespoons Marsala wine
40 savoiardi (ladyfinger) biscuits (about)
1 teaspoon cocoa powder, sifted
2 tablespoons powdered drinking chocolate

Zeppole

Zeppole are essentially doughnuts made from a ricotta dough, deep fried, and rolled in sugar. They are known by different names—*sfinci*, *sfinci di San Giuseppe*, and *sfingi*—and are most traditionally eaten at the religious festivals of Saint Joseph (patron of the poor) and Saint Martin (patron of wine). Going by how much wine is consumed during the Godfather movies, I believe a plate of zeppole should be a permanent addition to the table in honor of Saint Martin.

1. Combine the ricotta, ¼ cup of the sugar, egg and yolk, orange rind, flour, and baking powder and mix until smooth. Cover and refrigerate for 30 minutes.

2. Mix the remaining 1 cup of sugar and ground cinnamon together in a bowl. Set aside.

3. Pour enough oil into a medium saucepan to reach halfway up the sides and heat to 325°F.

4. Drop tablespoon-sized balls of the ricotta mixture into the oil in small batches. Fry until golden, turning often. Keep an eye on the oil—if it gets too hot, the zeppole will burn on the outside before they are cooked inside. The zeppole should fry gently, not aggressively, so adjust the heat as necessary.

5. Once cooked, drain on paper towels briefly and then add to the bowl of cinnamon sugar. Toss to coat. Serve hot.

SERVES 6 TO 8.

8 ounces fresh ricotta, drained
1¼ cup superfine sugar
1 egg plus 1 egg yolk
Finely grated rind of half an orange
¾ cup all-purpose flour
2 teaspoons baking powder
2 teaspoons ground cinnamon
Oil for frying

Panforte

Panforte means "strong bread," and just like the strong men in the Godfather movies, it is spicy, yet sweet, a little dense, dark, rich, and very intense. Traditionally served at Christmas, panfortes are often made and given as gifts to close friends.

1. Grease an 8-inch round springform pan with a little softened butter and line the base with parchment paper. Preheat oven to 300°F.

2. Mix together the figs, prunes, nuts, and peel. Sift the flour, cocoa powder, spices, and pepper over the fruit and nut mixture and fold to combine.

3. Melt the chocolate either in short bursts in a microwave, stirring between bursts, or in a bowl suspended over a saucepan of simmering water. Set aside.

4. Place the sugar and honey into a medium saucepan and cook over low-medium heat, stirring until the sugar dissolves. Bring to a boil and simmer without stirring until the mixture reaches 240°F on a candy thermometer, or until a small amount immediately forms a ball when dropped into cold water.

5. Pour the hot sugar mixture into the dry mix. Add the melted chocolate and mix everything together with a wooden spoon. Work quickly as the mixture will harden as it cools.

6. Spoon into your prepared pan and press the top with a spatula to compact and smooth the surface. Cook for 30 to 40 minutes, or until just firm. It will still seem a little wet in the middle, but it will harden as it cools, and you want a nice chewy texture rather than rock candy, so don't be tempted to overcook it.

7. Allow the panforte to cool completely, then run a sharp knife around the edge to free it from the sides of the pan. Carefully take it out of the pan, remove the base and parchment paper, and dust liberally all over with powdered sugar. If it's still a little soft, refrigerate until firm. The panforte is ready to eat now, but the flavor improves the longer it sits. Wrap tightly in plastic wrap and store in the refrigerator for up to 6 months.

8. To serve, slice into thin slices as needed. A little goes a long way.

SERVES 10.

7 ounces dried figs, chopped

7 ounces prunes, pitted and chopped

5 ounces almonds

4 ounces toasted hazelnuts, skins removed

½ ounce candied citrus peel, chopped

1 cup plain flour

2 tablespoons cocoa powder

1 teaspoon ground cinnamon

¼ teaspoon ground nutmeg

¼ teaspoon allspice

⅛ teaspoon ground cloves

½ teaspoon ground cardamom

½ teaspoon white pepper

2½ ounces dark chocolate, chopped

¾ cup sugar

½ cup honey

Powdered sugar for dusting

Italian Rum Cake

The classic Italian celebration cake, this cake has marked many special occasions in the Godfather movies, from Connie's wedding to the massive gold-embossed cake served at the party in Michael's honor in *The Godfather Part III.* Hyman Roth's birthday cake is especially symbolic. Adorned with the island of Cuba, it is cut and served at a meeting with all the crime bosses symbolizing Roth slicing up and sharing his wealth and Cuba's lucrative market for the consumption of all present. "I want all of you to eat your cake, so enjoy."

This cake is easiest to make in stages. The cakes can be made a day ahead as can the custard and syrup. Then all you need to do on the day you serve the cake is make the whipped cream and put it all together. In the Godfather movies this cake was made with lavish piped decorations, but you can decorate it any way you want. Adding the toasted almonds to the sides not only adds a lovely crunch and flavor to the cake, but also hides any imperfections—which takes away the stress of decorating perfection.

1. To make the cake: Preheat oven to 350°F. Grease and line the bottom of two 8-inch round cake tins with parchment. Grease the inside walls of the cake tins and add a few tablespoons of flour and shake the tins, rolling around so the flour sticks to the inside walls, coating the inside.

2. Put the eggs, sugar, and vanilla into a bowl and beat with an electric mixer with the whisk attachment until stiff and pale—about 8 minutes.

3. Sift the flour, corn starch, and baking powder into a large clean bowl, then sift again, right into the whipped egg mixture. Use a spatula to carefully fold the flours in and combine until smooth. Pour half of the cake batter into each tin. Tap gently onto the countertop (this gets rid of any air bubbles in the batter) and bake for 25 to 30 minutes, or until cakes have risen, are golden, and spring back when touched.

4. Remove from the oven and run a knife around the inside of the tins to help loosen the cakes, and immediately flip over onto a clean tea towel, keeping the tins upside down on the cakes. Let rest for 10 minutes like this, then remove the tins and peel off the parchment stuck to the bottom. Carefully turn over onto a wire rack to cool completely.

Continued on page 198 . . .

SERVES 10.

CAKE
6 eggs, room temperature
1 cup superfine sugar
2 teaspoons vanilla extract
½ cup all-purpose flour
1 cup corn starch
2½ teaspoons baking powder

RUM SYRUP
½ cup water
¼ cup rum
½ cup superfine sugar

VANILLA CUSTARD CREAM
½ cup superfine sugar
2 eggs
4 tablespoons corn starch
2 teaspoons vanilla extract
2 cups whole milk

CHOCOLATE CUSTARD CREAM
¼ cup superfine sugar
1 egg
1½ tablespoon corn starch
½ teaspoon vanilla extract
1 tablespoon cocoa powder
1 cup whole milk

WHIPPED CREAM
2 cups heavy or whipping cream
1 teaspoon vanilla extract
½ cup powdered sugar

DECORATION
1½ cups flaked almonds, toasted
150 grams dark chocolate, melted (optional)

5. To make the rum syrup: Mix the water, rum, and sugar in a small saucepan and heat on medium-high. Stir until all the sugar is dissolved. Bring to a boil and simmer for one minute. Set aside to cool.

6. To make the vanilla custard cream: Put the sugar, eggs, corn starch, and vanilla in a bowl and whisk until a smooth paste forms. Add the milk and whisk to combine. Transfer to a saucepan over medium heat and whisk continuously until thick—about 7 minutes.

7. Transfer to a large bowl. Allow to cool for a couple of minutes, then cover with plastic wrap, pressing directly onto the surface to stop a skin from forming. Refrigerate until cool.

8. For the chocolate custard cream: Make the chocolate custard cream the same way you made the vanilla custard cream, adding the cocoa powder with the other ingredients in the first step. As it is a small quantity, it will take less time to thicken, 4 to 5 minutes. Refrigerate until cool.

9. Both custard creams can be made a day in advance. They will thicken the longer they sit. Prior to using, beat briefly with a wooden spoon until smooth.

10. To assemble the cake: Use a serrated knife to cut the cakes crosswise in half, creating two layers out of each one. Place one layer onto a round board or plate you wish to serve on. As this is such a moist cake, it is best not to move it once assembled, so putting it on your cake stand or plate you plan on serving it is the best approach.

11. Drizzle or brush some rum syrup over the base layer, then add a layer of the vanilla custard cream. Top with another cake layer and drizzle with more rum syrup. Add a layer of chocolate custard cream, then another cake layer. Drizzle with more rum syrup, another layer of vanilla custard cream, then put the last cake layer on top. Refrigerate for 30 minutes.

12. To make the whipped cream: Whip the cream, vanilla, and powdered sugar with an electric beater until stiff peaks form.

13. Cover the entire cake with the whipped cream, piping rosettes to decorate as desired. Cover the sides with the flaked almonds. The easiest way to do this is just get handfuls of almonds and gently press around the edges evenly. If you want to write a message on top of the cake, put the melted chocolate into a piping bag fitted with a fine tip and pipe on top. This is purely optional. You can add fresh flowers, chocolate, strawberries, whatever you like.

14. Refrigerate for a few hours before serving so that everything sets.

Affogato

This is a classic Italian dessert and a great way to end a meal. You can't get simpler than coffee and ice cream (the liqueur is optional but recommended). What does "affogato" mean? Drowned. The ice cream drowned in the coffee. A bittersweet end.

1. Place 2 scoops of ice cream into 6 cups, glasses, or bowls. Drizzle each serving with 1 tablespoon liqueur and top with ¼ cup coffee.

2. Serve immediately.

SERVES 6.

12 scoops vanilla ice cream

6 tablespoons Frangelico, Amaretto, or other Italian liqueur (optional)

1½ cups espresso-strength coffee, hot

Measurement Conversion Charts

VOLUME

US	METRIC
⅛ teaspoon (tsp)	1 milliliter
1 teaspoon (tsp)	5 milliliter
1 tablespoon (tbsp)	15 milliliter
1 fluid ounce (fl. oz.)	30 milliliter
⅛ cup	50 milliliter
¼ cup	60 milliliter
⅓ cup	80 milliliter
3.4 fluid ounces (fl. oz.)	100 milliliter
½ cup	120 milliliter
⅔ cup	160 milliliter
¾ cup	180 milliliter
1 cup	240 milliliter
1 pint (2 cups)	480 milliliter
1 quart (4 cups)	0.95 liter

WEIGHT

US	METRIC
0.5 ounces (oz.)	14 grams
1 ounce (oz.)	28 grams
¼ pound (lb)	113 grams
⅓ pound (lb)	151 grams
½ pound (lb)	227 grams
1 pound (lb)	454 grams

TEMPERATURES

FAHRENHEIT	CELSIUS
200°	93.3°
212°	100°
250°	120°
275°	135°
300°	150°
325°	165°
350°	177°
400°	205°
425°	220°
450°	233°
475°	245°
500°	260°

ABOUT THE AUTHOR

Liliana Battle grew up in a Southern Italian family where the connection of food and family shaped her culinary passion. After appearing on MasterChef Australia, she published her popular debut cookbook *Easy Home Cooking Italian Style* followed by *Food for Sharing* and *The Sweet Life*, celebrating her heritage and recipes passed down through her family. She has catered everything from weddings to thousand-person corporate events, but it is cooking for her family that gives her the most pleasure. Liliana is a freelance writer and has featured on Food52, Lifestyle Food, and various other publications as well as her blog Liliana's Kitchen. She lives in a red dirt-mining town in the northwest of Australia with her husband, two sons, a grumpy King Charles Cavalier and a cheeky golden retriever. Liliana is an avid reader and has a special interest in ancient Rome. When she's not cooking or writing she dreams of riding a Vespa through the streets of an ancient Italian village with a basket load of fresh produce she picked up from the local market and the wind in her hair.

ABOUT THE PHOTOGRAPHER

Stacey Tyzzer discovered her fascination for photography and art at a young age and completed her bachelor of arts degree in applied visual imaging at the age of twenty-one. Originally from New Zealand, Stacey moved to the small mining town of Port Hedland in Western Australia where she established her own business, Locket Photography. She has photographed everything from large public events to weddings and births, and her images are featured in many publications. Stacey met Liliana Battle while photographing her cookbook *The Sweet Life*. She enjoys the perks that come with being a food photographer, namely being chief taste tester and being able to take containers of leftovers home for her husband Dane. A serious coffee addict and a globetrotter at heart, Stacey's aim is to photograph the world one café at a time.

AUTHOR ACKNOWLEDGMENTS

Like so many people, I am a massive Godfather fan and this book has been a joy to write. I am thankful to Insight Editions for entrusting me with such a monumental task: creating an authentic book that is worthy of being linked to this global phenomenon. I have loved every minute of writing it, not only because it's filled with so many recipes I cherish, love to eat and cook, but also because being Italian myself has given me a deeper, personal connection to the movies, and somehow has made me feel, in some small way, a part of the story. Thank you.

Thank you to my family who always support me and especially for putting up with the days and days of cooking and general upheaval writing a cookbook brings. Mum, thanks for all the family memories that culminate into my passion for food (also, thanks for being an awesome dishwasher during the shoot!). Jake and Jesse, cooking for you two is still my greatest pleasure. Jason, thanks for being you (and always coming home with wine just when I need it).

Thanks to my photographer, Stacey. Your dedication and willingness to spend way more time getting things the way I want than we really should just proves your professionalism and dedication to your craft (and extreme patience with me). I will miss our afternoon craziness once the light has gone and our Italian accents are at their thickest with movie quotes.

INSIGHT
EDITIONS

PO Box 3088
San Rafael, CA 94912
www.insighteditions.com

[f] Find us on Facebook: www.facebook.com/InsightEditions
[t] Follow us on Twitter: @insighteditions

Library of Congress Cataloging-in-Publication Data available.

ISBN: 978-1-68383-542-4

Publisher: Raoul Goff
Associate Publisher: Vanessa Lopez
Creative Director: Chrissy Kwasnik
Art Direction: Jon Glick
Design: Jon Glick and Katherine Yao
Project Editor: Kelly Reed
Editorial Assistant: Jeric Llanes
Production Editors: Jennifer Bentham and Elaine Ou
Senior Production Manager: Greg Steffen
Production Associate: Eden Orlesky

Illustrations by Katherine Yao

ROOTS of PEACE   🌳 REPLANTED PAPER

Insight Editions, in association with Roots of Peace, will plant two trees for each tree used in the manufac-
turing of this book. Roots of Peace is an internationally renowned humanitarian organization dedicated
to eradicating land mines worldwide and converting war-torn lands into productive farms and wildlife
habitats. Roots of Peace will plant two million fruit and nut trees in Afghanistan and provide farmers there
with the skills and support necessary for sustainable land use.

Manufactured in China by Insight Editions

10 9 8 7 6 5 4